COLLINS *rambler's guide*

KT-230-359

peak district

The Ramblers

HARVEY

roly smith

HarperCollins*Publishers*
77–85 Fulham Palace Road
London W6 8JB

The HarperCollins website address is:

www.**fire**and**water**.com

05 04 03 02

10 9 8 7 6 5 4 3

First published 2000

Series Editor Richard Sale
© in this edition HarperCollins*Publishers*
© in the text Roly Smith
© in the photographs Karen Frenkl
© in the maps Harvey Map Services Ltd., Doune, Perthshire
Walk profiles by Carte Blanche

The profiles given for each walk give an indication of the steepness and number of climbs on the route. The times on the profiles are calculated according to the Naismith formula which suggests one hour for each five map kilometres (three map miles) covered, together with an additional 30 minutes for each 300m (1,000ft) of ascent. For most walkers the formula underestimates the time taken for several reasons. Firstly few walkers complete a walk as a route march; secondly, there is no allowance for the terrain crossed, and it is easier to walk quickly over short grass than rough moor; thirdly, there is no allowance for stopping to admire the view, places of interest etc; and finally there is no allowance for rest stops. Rest stops tend to become both longer and more frequent as the walk length increases, so the time error increases as walks get longer. Please check yourself against the times on the first walks you attempt to gauge the time you will take on others.

ISBN 0 00 220116 X

Designed and produced by Drum Enterprises Ltd.
Printed and bound in Great Britain by Scotprint

CONTENTS

How to use this book

This book contains route maps and descriptions for 30 walks. Each walk is graded (see p.3) and areas of interest are indicated by symbols (see below). For each walk particular points of interest are denoted by a capital letter both in the text and on the map (where the letter appears in a red box). In the text the route descriptions are prefixed by lower-case letters. We recommend that you read the whole description, including the tinted box at the start of each walk, before setting out.

Key to maps

P	Car park	———+———+———	Powerline	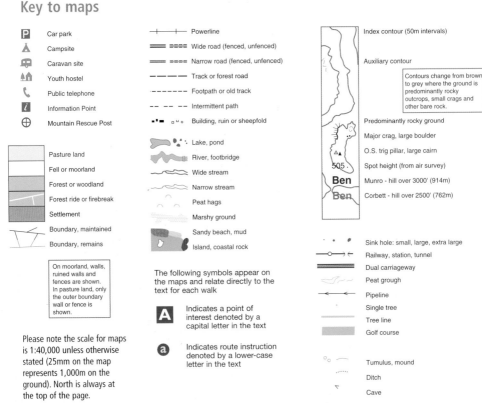	Index contour (50m intervals)
Å	Campsite	▬▬▬ ▭▭▭▭	Wide road (fenced, unfenced)		
	Caravan site	▬▬▬ ════	Narrow road (fenced, unfenced)		Auxiliary contour
	Youth hostel	— — — —	Track or forest road		
☎	Public telephone	- - - - - - -	Footpath or old track		
i	Information Point	-- -- --	Intermittent path		
⊕	Mountain Rescue Post	▪▪■ ▫ ◡ ○	Building, ruin or sheepfold		Predominantly rocky ground

Contours change from brown to grey where the ground is predominantly rocky with outcrops, small crags and other bare rock.

Major crag, large boulder

O.S. trig pillar, large cairn

505 · Spot height (from air survey)

Ben Munro - hill over 3000' (914m)

Ben Corbett - hill over 2500' (762m)

	Lake, pond
	River, footbridge
	Wide stream
	Narrow stream
	Peat hags
	Marshy ground
	Sandy beach, mud
	Island, coastal rock

	Pasture land
	Fell or moorland
	Forest or woodland
	Forest ride or firebreak
	Settlement
	Boundary, maintained
	Boundary, remains

On moorland, walls, ruined walls and fences are shown. In pasture land, only the outer boundary wall or fence is shown.

The following symbols appear on the maps and relate directly to the text for each walk

A Indicates a point of interest denoted by a capital letter in the text

ⓐ Indicates route instruction denoted by a lower-case letter in the text

· · • Sink hole: small, large, extra large

—○—→← Railway, station, tunnel

▬▬▬ Dual carriageway

Peat grough

—←—←— Pipeline

· Single tree

Tree line

Golf course

○ Tumulus, mound

Ditch

Cave

Please note the scale for maps is 1:40,000 unless otherwise stated (25mm on the map represents 1,000m on the ground). North is always at the top of the page.

0 Kilometres   1   2

0 Miles   1

Key to symbols

The walks in this book are graded from 1–5 according to the level of difficulty, with 1 being the easiest and 5 the most difficult. We recommend that walks graded 4 or higher (or grade 3 where indicated) should only be undertaken by experienced walkers who are competent in the use of map and compass and who are aware of the difficulties of the terrain they will encounter. The use of detailed maps is recommended for all routes.

At the start of each walk there is a series of symbols that indicate particular areas of interest associated with the route.

 Birdlife

 Good views

 Other wildlife

 Historical interest

 Wild flowers

 Woodland

INTRODUCTION

The Inland Island

The Peak District has often been described as an island, surrounded as it is by the vast, sprawling conurbations of northern England and the Midlands. Half the population of the country, it is said, lives within 96.5km/60 miles of its centre, and the National Park Authority estimates that it receives an astonishing 22 million visits each year. Only one other National Park in the world receives more visitors than that, but Mount Fuji in Japan is a *proper* National Park, owned by the nation and virtually uninhabited.

For in addition to those enormous number of day visitors, most of whom come by car from the surrounding towns and cities, about 38,000 people also live and work within the Peak District – making it probably the most pressurised National Park in Europe as well. But it has always been a vital, last green open space and lung for those teeming visitors, and its recreational importance to them can hardly be overestimated.

Escaping the crowds – Stanage Edge looking south

Doing the Pennine Way on
Bleaklow

Yet it is still possible, even on a Bank Holiday Monday when half the world seems to descend on honeypots like Bakewell and Castleton, to get away from the crowds in the 1,437km²/555 sq.-mile National Park. An unrivalled network of around 2,253km/1,400 miles of public rights of way, plus easy 'leisure routes' such as the Tissington and High Peak Trails which have been developed from derelict railway lines, and over 207km²/80 sq. miles of open access on the northern moors, make the Peak perhaps the most accessible National Park for the walker.

And there is an unrivalled range of walking available, from gentle, riverside strolls in the sylvan limestone dales or across the limestone plateau on one of the railway trails, to tough moorland treks across some of the most difficult walking country in Britain on those northern access moors. Few places in Britain have such an infinite variety of walking opportunities in such a small area.

That island analogy also applies to the Peak's topography. It rises proudly from the surrounding lowland plains as the first outpost of Highland Britain, a fact which is perhaps seen most graphically as you travel across one of the pitch-black moorland roads in the north, west or east of the National Park, when the street lights of the encircling cities glow below you like a field of stars.

The highest point – somewhere in the middle of the boggy plateau of Kinder Scout north of Edale – is only 636m/2,088ft above the sea, but the limestone plateau in the south also averages over 300m/1,000ft. You can have no doubt as you enter the National Park from the south at Ashbourne, from the

White Peak limestone plateau
near Wardlow Mires

Winter landscape of the Dark Peak

west via Leek or from the east from Sheffield or Chesterfield, that you are entering hill country. As an early 18th century traveller famously remarked as he climbed up the Buxton road from Ashbourne's cobbled market place, 'at the summit of the hill, it was a top coat colder.'

Despite that relatively modest altitude, the hills of the Peak District can create weather conditions which are as severe as anywhere in Britain – especially in winter. There are many apocryphal tales of walkers under-estimating the seriousness of places like Kinder Scout, including legions of Pennine Wayfarers who have turned back, utterly demoralised, hours after starting out on the first leg across Kinder from Edale. It's worth remembering that the Peak lies on the same latitude as Labrador and Siberia and that a mile on the cloying, glutinous peat of the northern moors is equivalent to about five miles anywhere else, in terms of the amount of energy which has to be expended to make progress.

John Derry, in his classic 1926 guidebook *Across the Derbyshire Moors* described such terrain perfectly: '... the most featureless, disconsolate, bog-quaking, ink-oozing moor

Thor's Cave, Manifold Valley

you ever saw.' Yet these forbidding moors have a large band of aficionados, affectionately and accurately known as 'bog-trotters,' who perform prodigious feats of mileage across this most unpromising yet challenging of surfaces.

Topographically speaking, the Peak District has a spilt personality. The limestone White Peak, which occupies the central and southern area of the National Park, is a soft, gentle landscape. Lushly-vegetated, steep-sided dales strewn with wildflowers in the summer and watered by crystal-clear streams like the Dove, Manifold and Lathkill, dissect the broad, rolling limestone plateau, where miles of drystone walls criss-cross the emerald meadows like a net holding down the billowing landscape.

In direct counterpoint to the White Peak, and enclosing it to the north, west and east in an upturned horseshoe, is the starker gritstone Dark Peak. The base rock here is millstone grit, a coarse, abrasive sandstone which outcrops in the famous Peakland eastern 'edges' – short but steep escarpments which look down on the valley of the Derwent. Beyond the tor-topped edges, the sombre heather and peat-clad moorlands rise to the highest ground in the National Park, at Kinder, Bleaklow and Black Hill.

The limestone of the White Peak is the oldest rock which is exposed in the area – the very skeleton of the landscape. Laid down under a shallow, tropical sea during the Carboniferous period about 350 million years ago, the limestone consists of the remains of millions upon millions of microscopic sea creatures which lived and died in that ancient sea, at a time when what is now the Peak District was close to the Equator. You can still see the remains of these fossilised land-building skeletons in the stones of the drystone walls, or in gateposts and the typical 'squeezer' stiles, where the screw-like stems of crinoids (sea lilies) have been polished by years of abrasion.

On the edges of this tropical lagoon, harder limestones built up in reefs, just as they are doing today in places like Australia's Great Barrier Reef. This harder reef limestone gives us the few real peaks in the area, like the upstanding rock pinnacles of Dovedale and the Manifold, and the isolated ridge-peaks of Chrome and Parkhouse Hills in the upper Dove.

Bleak peaty summit of Bleaklow

Typical heather moorland of the Dark Peak (Owler Tor)

There were occasional volcanic interludes in this tranquil tropical paradise, the results of which can be seen in places like Tideswell Dale, where the black basalt outcrops, and it also resulted in the veins of lead and fluorspar which permeated through the limestone to endow the Peak with its mineral wealth, which was so economically-important in the past.

Later meltwater from Ice Age glaciers gouged out the steep-sided limestone dales, and the slightly acidic rainwater took advantage of the bedding planes and cracks in the limestone to form the caves of the White Peak, such as Thor's Cave in the Manifold, Reynard's Cave in Dovedale, and the famous show caverns at Castleton, Matlock, and Buxton.

Later during the same geological epoch, the limestone was buried under coarse sediments, grits and mudbanks which spread out in great deltas from huge rivers flowing from the north. These darker sediments overlaid the limestone in vast quantities, and after aeons of time were solidified into the shales, sandstones and gritstones of the Dark Peak, later to be pushed up into the 'Derbyshire Dome.'

Whereas the limestone was porous and dissolved in water, the gritstones of the Dark Peak were impervious and poorly-drained. So any vegetation which grew on the surface, like sphagnum moss, bilberry and heather, quickly rotted down to form immense layers of peat, creating the bleak moorland landscapes of today.

The major rivers of the north and eastern Peak, such as the Derwent and Wye, exploited the shale valleys which form the border between the limestone and gritstone, and now flow in broad, tree-filled valleys to join the Trent and eventually reach the North Sea. The Goyt and Dane drain the western side of the Dark Peak, where the topography is somewhat more complex and folded than in the east, and eventually flow into the Mersey and the Irish Sea.

Arbor Low

The White Peak was the first area of the Peak to be permanently inhabited by Man following the retreat of the glaciers about 10,000 years ago. But the earliest evidence of human activity in the area are the isolated 'microliths' – tiny flakes of flint – which are often found in the peat of the Dark Peak moors, providing evidence of the hunting activities of Mesolithic (Middle Stone Age) man.

Remains of Neolithic (New Stone Age) man have been found in rock shelters and caves in many White Peak dales, including Dowel Dale, Cales Dale and the Manifold Valley. But the most obvious and spectacular of the Stone Age remains in the Peak is the stone circle and henge monument of Arbor Low, near Youlgreave, sometimes known as 'the Stonehenge of the North.' Arbor Low, with its ring of prostrate, weathered limestone slabs enclosed within the steep bank and ditch of its encircling henge, still manages to exert an aura of mystery and awe which its over-interpreted southern counterpart has completely lost.

Standing on the edge of the Bronze Age burial mound which was superimposed on the rim of the henge, at 375m/1,230ft above the sea, and looking round the vast sweep of the White Peak landscape, the sense of continuity with the ancient past is very strong. Looking to the south east, the spindly crown of beeches which tops Minninglow, a Neolithic chambered tomb, can just be seen, while on almost every other hilltop, there is the little raised bump of a Bronze Age tumulus. These high points were obviously important to our prehistoric ancestors.

In nearly every case, these tumuli carry the suffix 'low' from the Old English 'hlaw' for burial mound. (It is one of the many paradoxes of the Peak that 'low' should usually denote a high point. Another is that despite the name, there are few real 'peaks' in the area). There are estimated to be as many as 500 of these barrows in the Peak, most of which were rather clumsily excavated by Victorian antiquaries like Thomas Bateman of Middleton-by-Youlgreave.

The artefacts recovered reveal a relatively high population of simple farmers, and their hut circles and field systems show that they favoured the thin soils of the Dark Peak above the river valleys of the Derwent and Wye. Archaeologists now believe that this area, which is now almost all under rank moor grass and heather, may have been over-farmed in this

Peveril Castle and Mam Tor

Eyam Hall

period and this, added to a deterioration in the climate, resulted in people moving back to the White Peak area in succeeding generations.

The major evidence of the Iron Age in the Peak is found in the eight so-called hillforts which encircle prominent hills such as Mam Tor, above Castleton at the head of the Hope Valley, Fin Cop, above Monsal Dale, and Burr Tor, near Great Hucklow. Once thought to be entirely defensive structures, many of these embanked enclosures are now believed to have had a more peaceful purpose, and may have been summer sheilings used to keep watch over grazing herds of livestock. They were certainly also tribal meeting places of tribes like the Pecsaete, or 'people of the Peak,' just like the henge monuments of Neolithic times, and at places like Mam Tor, surely one of the most impressive hillforts in the Pennines, evidence of their hut circles has been found.

The Romans were attracted to the Peak District because of its abundant supplies of lead, and it is thought that the most significant monument they left behind, the fort of *Navio* at Brough in the Hope Valley, was built to protect their lead mining interests. The lead mining centre of *Ludutarum*, named on Roman pigs of lead, has still to be conclusively identified. There was another fort at *Melandra* near Glossop, and Buxton had a short-lived fame as a Roman spa town, known as *Aquae Arnemetiae*.

The so-called 'Dark Ages' left a rich legacy in the Peak District, with the finest collection of Celtic crosses outside Northumbria adorning the churchyards at Bakewell, Eyam, Hope and Ilam. A 'burh' in the neighbourhood of Bakewell was the scene in 920 AD of a major 'summit' meeting between King Edward the Elder and the kings of Danish Northumbria, Wales and Scotland.

Magpie Mine near Sheldon

Red campion in Miller's Dale

After the Norman Conquest, much of the northern part of the Peak District was commandeered as the Royal Forest of the Peak – a 104km²/40 sq. mile hunting preserve in which kings and princes pursued game for sport. The forest was administered from William Peveril's castle on the rocky knoll between Peak Cavern and Cave Dale above Castleton. Castleton was a planned medieval township which took its name from Peveril's fortified headquarters, and other towns and villages which blossomed with the granting of market rights during this period were Bakewell, Tideswell, Hartington and Monyash.

The great age of re-building created the well-known mansions of Haddon, Eyam Hall, Lyme Park and the original Chatsworth, as wealthy landowners sought to demonstrate their power and wealth. The former open landscape of the Peak was gradually enclosed as these landowners took in more and more land from the moorland for cultivation, creating the familiar pattern of drystone-walled fields we see today. Chief among these landowners were the Earls and later Dukes of Devonshire from Chatsworth, and the Dukes of Rutland from Haddon.

That mineral wealth, especially of lead, which had brought the Romans to the Peak was another major source of income to the landed gentry, and during the 18th and 19th centuries, the lead mining industry of the White Peak became very important. Even today, the landscape of the limestone plateau is littered with the remains of the workings of 't'owd man' as the lead miners, who usually doubled as farmers, were known. The best-known, and best-preserved, former lead

July in Lathkilldale

mine is Magpie Mine, near Sheldon, now run as a field study centre. During the early 19th century, there were over 2,000 lead miners in the White Peak area, and the industry made a significant contribution to the economic wealth and culture of the area.

Deserted homestead, Coplowdale

The Industrial Revolution of the late 18th and early 19th century only lightly touched the rivers and valleys of the Peak, and cotton mills like those at Cressbrook, Cromford and Litton employed child labour in the new industries. After the gradual spread of turnpike roads across the Peakland hills came the railways. Among the earliest in the Golden Age of railway building was the Cromford and High Peak Railway, which was built across the 305-m/1,000-ft limestone plateau in 1830 after originally and somewhat ambitiously being planned as a canal! The Midland line followed 30 years later.

Later still came the reservoirs to slake the insatiable thirst of the citizens of the new industrial cities – like Manchester, Sheffield, Stoke and Derby which sprang up around the edges

Hidden waterfall near Eyam

Moorhen in the River Bradford

of the Peak. The most famous of these are the three which flooded the upper section of the Derwent Valley – the Howden, Derwent and Ladybower, and the five which filled the Longdendale Valley in the north of the National Park, whose water went to the boom towns of Manchester and Stockport. The fast-expanding populations of those surrounding industrial cities had traditionally used the Peak District for their recreation at weekends, but the Enclosure Movement had robbed them of their access to many of the highest and wildest moors, which were strictly preserved by the new landowners for shooting grouse. A huge pressure for access to these forbidden moors built up during the great Depression of the early 1930s, and culminated in the famous Mass Trespass on Kinder Scout in April, 1932.

The pressure for better access was one of the most important catalysts which saw the creation of the Peak District National Park – the first in Britain – in April, 1951. Another was the urgent need to conserve the last remaining green space in the south Pennines from unsuitable industrial and residential development. Despite its industrial surroundings and past, the Peak District has long been a haven for wildlife, a further reason for its urgent designation as a National Park.

As stated above, the Peak District stands at the crossroads of Britain, at the meeting place of the Highland and Lowland zones. This means that it provides the southernmost habitat for a number of northern species of wildlife, such as the cloudberry and mountain hare, and the northernmost habitat for some southern species, such as the nettle-leaved bellflower and the nuthatch.

This, together with the wide variety of geology and landscape types already described, makes it a paradise for the naturalist, who can see an infinite variety of wildlife and plantlife in a very small area – sometimes even in a single dale.

The limestone dales are by far the richest wildlife habitats in the Peak District, and the 350ha/865 acre Derbyshire Dales National Nature Reserve, set up in 1972, is regarded as one of the top five NNRs in the country by English Nature. It comprises parts of Lathkill, Monk's, Cressbrook, Biggin, Long

Peak District dew pond near Little Hucklow

and Hay Dales and is visited by over 300,000 people annually. Specialities of these limestone dales include the beautiful, purplish-blue flowers of Jacob's Ladder, found in the upper reaches of Lathkill Dale, and the rare and lovely pink-flowered shrub mezereon, which is found in woodland in Lathkill Dale and Dovedale. Over 50 species of wildflowers and herbs can be identified per $1m^2/10.76ft^2$ in the lime-rich grasslands of these limestone dales.

Dovedale's ashwoods are nationally important, although surprisingly, this most famous of all the limestone dales is not part of the Derbyshire Dales NNR. Most of the dale, with its striking limestone crags, is however in the safe hands of the National Trust. The Derbyshire and Staffordshire Wildlife Trusts also have important reserves in the Wye and Manifold Valleys.

Most of the common British mammals can be found in the limestone dales, including the recent welcome reappearance of the otter. Birdlife includes the ubiquitous dipper and grey wagtail in and around the crystal-clear rivers many of which, like the Lathkill, Hamps and Manifold, can disappear into underground channels in the summer. Lathkill Dale is also famous for its butterflies, which include the rare northern brown argus, white letter hairstreak, and dingy skipper.

The Dark Peak, in contrast, supports a much less varied and rich wildlife. The exceptions are the exciting moorland birds of prey, such as the peregrine falcon, the diminutive merlin, the dashing goshawk, and the graceful hen harrier, all of which are enjoying a revival after many years of persecution.

The main agents in the persecution of these magnificent raptors were those same gamekeepers who tried to keep ramblers off the moors, because heather moorland is the preferred habitat for the red grouse, whose 'go back, go back, back, back' call is a constant accompaniment to a moorland walk in the Dark Peak.

However, it should always be remembered that we owe the rich tapestry of royal-hued heather which is one of the joys of a moorland walk in late summer to those gamekeepers, who manage these moors almost exclusively for the grouse which their masters delight to shoot after the 'Glorious Twelfth' of August.

In the rocky cloughs (steep-sided valleys) of the moorland streams, the clear song of the ring ouzel or mountain

blackbird can often be heard, while golden plover and curlew are the most common waders seen or heard on the moor tops. And in a snowless winter, an increasingly common sight especially on the Eastern Moors is the conspicuous white coat of the mountain hare, re-introduced to the area during the 19th century for sporting purposes.

White or Dark, the Peak District has something for everybody, and active walkers will find that they can soon escape from the crowds and experience the delights of this paradoxical 'Inland Island' at first hand.

Peter's Rock, Ravensdale, White Peak

DOVEDALE

START/FINISH:
Dovedale car park (toilets), near Thorpe

DISTANCE:
11km/7 miles

APPROXIMATE TIME:
Allow 4–5 hours

HIGHEST POINT:
Ilam Moor Lane, 304m/995ft

MAP:
OS Outdoor Leisure Sheet 24, The White Peak

REFRESHMENTS:
At the Dovedale car park and Milldale

ADVICE:
Easy dale walking on an engineered path, then some field and lane walking

WILDLIFE INTEREST:
Dipper, grey wagtail, kingfisher, wheatear. Rainbow and brown trout, lamprey, crayfish. Ash, mezereon, rockrose, thyme

Dovedale is the triumphant crescendo of the Peak District dales symphony – a melodramatic medley of soaring pinnacles, caves, and natural arches which spring from the cool ash woodland. Through all of this the Dove, which Walton dubbed 'the Princess of rivers' burbles contentedly. No wonder that this is the most popular dale of them all, but it is wise to choose the time of your visit carefully if you wish to avoid the summertime queues at the Stepping Stones.

A Dovedale (Car Park) 146507

The rock formations of Dovedale were formed from the same reef limestone which forms the sharply-pointed hills of Chrome and Parkhouse at its head. The river, which today seems incapable of the creation of such monumental rock architecture, carved out this canyon-like gorge when it was swelled by the powerful erosive meltwaters of Ice Age glaciers. These cut down through fissures and faults in the rock leaving the harder limestones standing isolated. Bunster Hill and Thorpe Cloud, the twin sentinels which guard the entrance to the Dovedale gorge, were even harder to wear down and now stand as proud portals to the drama beyond.

Such is the popularity of the walk through Dovedale that the National Park Authority, in partnership with Derbyshire and Staffordshire County Councils and the owners, the National Trust, have an almost continuous programme of restoration and renewal on the footpath through to Hartington.

Dovedale and Thorpe Cloud

Wild thyme

a Leave the car park and turn right past the water company's flow meter and walk up the road which follows the west bank beneath Bunster Hill to the famous Stepping Stones.

B   The Stepping Stones 151513

This is one of the most popular places in the entire Peak District National Park. The series of square-cut stones which cross the river here are not particularly ancient; they were erected in Victorian times when there were donkeys stationed here for hire to take you further into the dale. Polished by millions of pairs of boots and shoes, the Stepping Stones now have a fine patina which shows up the crinoid fossils beautifully as you watch where you are putting your feet!

b Once across the river, the path passes through a squeezer stile and winds up on natural rock steps to the first major viewpoint in the dale, Lover's Leap.

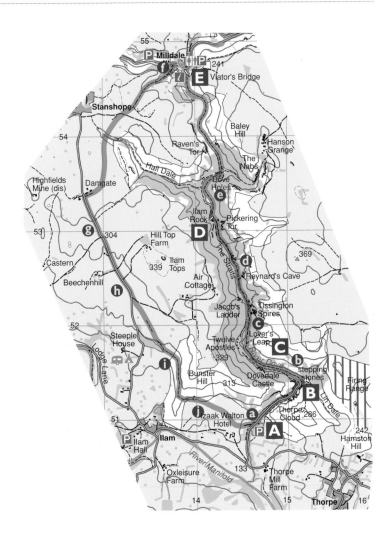

C   Lover's Leap viewpoint 145517

This is a fine place to study the lower portion of the dale. Opposite, rising out of the ashwoods, are the rock pinnacles known as the Twelve Apostles. Downstream, the bulk of Bunster Hill partly blocks the view of Thorpe Cloud. The thickly-wooded nature of this part of the dale often obscures the views of the natural rocks – a relatively recent phenomenon since grazing has been reduced in the dales. Turn-of-the-century photographs show much more of the rock formations, which is another reason why a winter or spring visit to Dovedale can often be much more rewarding.

c Steps lead down through the trees from Lover's Leap past the barely visible, yew-clad needles of Tissington Spires (right). A few steps further on, and away to the right will be seen the natural arch of Reynard's Cave (the actual cave is beyond the natural arch). The more adventurous will want to scramble up the steep slope to reach it, but it is slippery and eroded, so take care.

d Now the dale walls crowd in on either side to the section known as The Straits. Here the footpath has been raised above the level of the river, which is often subject to flooding at this point. The path passes under the Lion's Head Rock (use your imagination!) and then the dale opens out slightly where a footbridge crosses to Ilam Rock.

Please note: time taken calculated according to the Naismith formula (see p.2)

Pickering Tor, Dovedale

D   Ilam Rock and Pickering Tor 142531

These delicate fingers of rock gesticulating to each other across the Dove are one of the scenic highlights of the dale. Amazingly, the 25m high leaning finger of Ilam Rock has several rock climbing routes up its precipitous sides, while Pickering Tor has a gaping cave at its foot.

e   The path now swings east opposite Hall Dale to pass the impressively-yawning water-worn cavities known as Dove Holes. Beyond here, the riverside path passes a number of weirs before running under the impressive cliff of Raven's Tor. A gentle meadowland path now takes you to the hamlet of Milldale, reached by crossing the narrow Viator's Bridge.

E   Milldale and Viator's Bridge 139547

The former packhorse bridge now known as Viator's gets its name from a passage in Izaak Walton's *The Compleat Angler*, first published in 1653. 'Do you use to Travel with wheelbarrows in this country?' asks Viator of his companion, Piscator, when they come across it. '... why a mouse can hardly go over it; 'Tis not two fingers broad'. The water mill which gave Milldale its name is long gone, and most of the traffic in this remote little spot now consists of walkers. A small barn near the bridge serves as a National Trust information point, telling the story of their Dovedale estate.

f   From the Viator's bridge turn left up a narrow road; 46–90m/50–100 yards up on the left a signposted footpath leads up the bank. There is a squeezer stile about 27m/30 yards up the path followed by three more stiles – keep the wall on your left. At the fourth squeezer stile go straight on, keeping the wall on the right. A fifth squeezer stile takes you onto the lane leading to Stanshope Pasture. Turn right down the lane and then left after about 46m/50 yards onto Ilam Moor Lane.

g   Ilam Moor Lane is followed for about 800m/½ mile, and takes you over the high point of the walk (304m/995ft). This ridgetop lane enjoys extensive views across the Lower Manifold Valley to the right towards Throwley, with Mere Hill prominent. To the left, Dovedale is hidden by the rounded hills of Ilam Tops, with their summit tumulus of Ilam Tops Low.

h   The unfenced road to Ilam Tops soon appears on the left. The footpath takes you over a wall stile. Follow the direction of the signpost over the farm drive to another wall stile; the route then passes an old quarry on the right.

Milldale and Viator's Bridge

i The path now traverses the lower slopes of Bunster Hill, which is prominent to the left, and crosses an area of strip lynchets and ridge-and-furrow, indicative of medieval cultivation systems. The estate village of Ilam appears below ahead and to the right, but you continue to contour around the slopes of Bunster Hill maintaining height until you reach a saddle, where you descend to a stile.

j Two more stiles lead around the back of the Izaak Walton Hotel, from where you bear left to emerge at a stile opposite your starting point at the Dovedale car park.

PILSBURY CASTLE

Hartington is the 'capital' of the Upper Dove Valley, and its spacious square, fine buildings and lovely church give it the air of a much bigger place. This walk goes up the valley from Hartington and has as its objective one of the most interesting medieval sites in the Peak – a splendidly-sited motte-and-bailey castle which commands the reaches of the Upper Dove from a natural defensive position at Pilsbury.

A Hartington 128604

The prosperous, urbane air of Hartington probably dates from as long ago as 1203, when it was the first Peak District town to be granted a charter to hold a weekly market. The ruling family then were the De Ferriers, whose ancestors probably founded the solid little Perpendicular-towered hilltop church of St. Giles, which now dates mainly from the 14th century. The modern Market Hall, now a shop, dates from 1836. Another of Hartington's fine old buildings is the early 17th century Jacobean-style Hartington Hall to the east of the village centre. This is surely one of the grandest youth hostels in Britain, and claims that one of its earliest 'bed-nights' was none other than Bonnie Prince Charlie, on his way to Derby in his ill-fated bid for the English throne in 1745.

Fossils in wall (including crinoids)

Hartington YHA – Hartington Hall

Old photographs show Hartington's Market Square bustling with traders and travelling shows with exotic animals such as bears on display. Today, the square is mostly occupied by visitors and their cars, many of whom use in as a base for walking in the Upper Dove Valley.

a From the restored village mere (pond), follow Dig Street northwards. After the drive leading to Moathall turn right onto a track which rises to meet Hide Lane.

b You are now faced with a choice of routes. You can either take the footpath down to the valley road north which leads to Pilsbury, via Banktop, Ludwell Farm and Parks Barn. At Pilsbury, where the road turns sharp right, take the footpath on the left which soon leads to Pilsbury Castle.

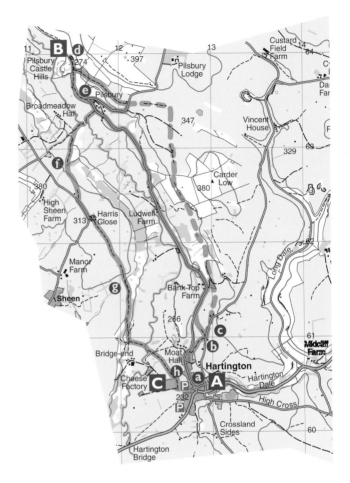

c Alternatively, turn left onto Hide Lane and where it takes a right-hand bend, take the stile to the left which is next to a barn. Follow the footpath through a series of stiles traversing below Carder Low, which rises to just over 380m/1,247ft above the limestone outcrops to the right. Where the path descends to a crossroads take the path on the left (signposted to Pilsbury and Crowdecote) and continue over a lane and after 400m/¼ mile you reach Pilsbury Castle.

d Either route gives extensive and expanding views towards Pilsbury and the reef limestone peaks of Chrome and Parkhouse Hills at the head of the Upper Dove valley. Across the valley to the left the 380m/1,247ft table-topped Sheen Hill is prominent.

Pilsbury Castle Hills towards the Upper Dove

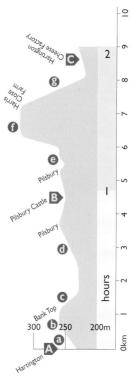

B   Pilsbury Castle 114638

Guarded by an upstanding crag of reef limestone, Pilsbury is a classic example of an early Norman motte-and-bailey castle. When originally built in the 11th or 12th centuries, it would have had a wooden stockade around the exterior embankment of the bailey, and the motte would have been crowned by further stockading and probably a wooden watchtower. It may well have been the original administrative centre for the De Ferriers family's Dove Valley estates, but by the 13th century, the De Ferriers, Earls of Lancaster by this time, had moved their headquarters down the valley to Hartington. Another school of thought suggests that Pilsbury may have been constructed during the 12th century civil wars between Stephen and Maltilda.

The name of the site also suggests that the naturally defensive site, controlling the length of the valley, may have been utilised even earlier.

e   Return to Pilsbury and turn right on the footpath beside a wall which descends to the footbridge over the River Dove and ascends the other bank by the green lane which was a former Salt Way which led from Cheshire to the towns east of the

Pennines. To the right stands the attractive ruins of Jacobean Broadmeadow Hall (no access).

f Take the stile to the left opposite the entrance to the hall, and climb diagonally up the slope to reach the road which runs beneath the top of Sheen Hill ahead. Turn left on the road until you reach Harris Close Farm, where you leave the road and continue straight ahead through the farmyard and follow the embanked wall to your right which descends above the escarpment towards a plantation.

g Keep on the path which runs through the upper edge of the plantation and then descends through scrub to a stile. There is a fine view of Hartington, with the tower of the church prominent, down to the left. Bear right here and then

Sheen Hill from above Pilsbury showing Broadmeadow Hall

on reaching a path crossroads turn left through a series of stiles which eventually bring you to the forecourt of the Hartington cheese factory.

C Hartington Cheese Factory 125604

Many visitors to Hartington will go away with one of village's specialities – a piece of Stilton Cheese. This 'King of English Cheeses' is made at Hartington's Dairy Crest Cheese Factory, and can only be made in Derbyshire, Leicestershire or Nottinghamshire – and Hartington just 800m/½ mile from the Staffordshire border, just qualifies. Tours of the factory are sometimes arranged.

h At the access road to the factory, turn left to return to the centre of the village and your starting point.

THE PEAKS OF THE UPPER DOVE

START/FINISH:
Longnor Market Square Car Park. Buses to Buxton and Hartington, and infrequently to Leek

DISTANCE:
13–14.5km/8–9 miles

APPROXIMATE TIME:
Allow about 4–5 hours

HIGHEST POINT:
Chrome Hill, 430m/1,411ft

MAP:
OS Outdoor Leisure Sheet 24, White Peak

REFRESHMENTS:
Pubs and cafe in Longnor, pub in Earl Sterndale

ADVICE:
A stiff climb to a narrow limestone ridge (take special care here), not for vertigo-sufferers, then field paths and lanes and another stiff climb to High Wheeldon. Also take care on road sections

WILDLIFE INTEREST:
Limestone fossils, crinoids etc. Skylark, lapwing, curlew, wheatear. Badger, fox, weasel, hare, rabbit

Many visitors come away from the Peak District disappointed that they have seen no real 'peaks' in the dictionary sense of sharply-pointed hills. But this absorbing stroll around the hills of the Upper Dove Valley from Longnor reveals the finest of the few real peaks in the Peak District. Chrome, Parkhouse and High Wheeldon Hills really live up to the name, and provide exciting scrambling and marvellous views.

A Longnor 088649

The gritstone village of Longnor on a narrow ridge between the Dove and the Manifold clusters around its cobbled Market Square and the gabled 19th century Market Hall, which still exhibits a scale of tolls for traders on its walls and is now a craft centre. Longnor stands at the junction of a number of formerly important turnpike roads which crossed the Staffordshire moors, and Longnor people are keen to point out that the postal address of nearby Leek was once 'near Longnor'. Another indication of Longnor's former importance is that it still manages to support four pubs in a village with a population of just over 400.

a Start from the cobbled Market Square on Longnor. Facing the Market Hall walk up the charming little alley of Chapel Street which is on your left. At the top of Chapel Street at the junction with Church Street, cross over and bear left for a short distance but not as far as the Buxton Road. Take the lane between ruined farm buildings and after about 90m/100 yards there is a signed footpath up the bank on the right.

Parkhouse Hill in Dowal Dale

Looking towards High Wheeldon from between Longnor and Crowdecote at Top o' th' Edge

Follow the wall crossing over two stiles until you reach a third from which there is a fine view across the valley to the hills of the Upper Dove.

B   The Upper Dove Hills (viewpoint 088653)

It's hard to conceive on a winter's day in North Staffordshire, but the upstanding hills of the Upper Dove were formed under conditions very similar to those that exist today on the Great Barrier Reef, off the eastern coast of Australia. All that was around 350 million years ago, of course, when Britain was much closer to the Equator, and this area was submerged under a warm, shallow tropical sea. On the edge of this shimmering sea, coral reefs built up, eventually forming the more resistant limestone from which the present Chrome, Parkhouse and High Wheeldon hills were eventually created. The sharp divide of Dowel Dale across the valley is thought to have been an underwater inter-coral channel and so has been there since the hills were formed.

This so-called reef limestone is also responsible for the isolated pinnacles and crags of the lower reaches of Dovedale downstream.

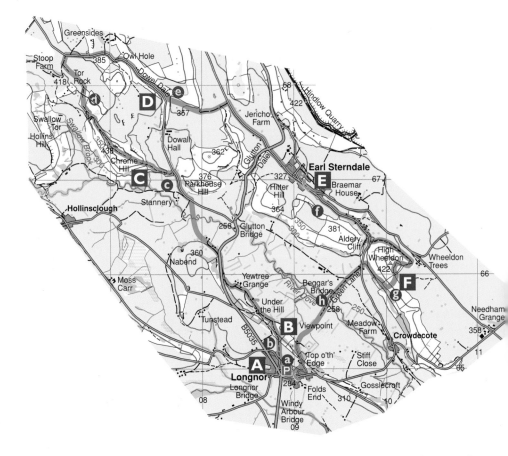

b Follow the path down the bank and take the farm track (not the more obvious track) which leads to Yew Tree Grange, following it to a road junction (B5053). Turn right, and just before the road starts a sharp descent to Glutton Bridge, turn left on the lane to Dove Bank. Go through a narrow gate above Dove Bank Cottage and through a stile to reach a wooden footbridge over the Dove. You now join the minor road leading up into Dowel Dale, turning left under the serrated shadow of Parkhouse Hill (372m/1,221ft) with its attendant the Sugar Loaf, and soon bearing right, passing the path to Stannery Farm.

c After about 90m/100 yards you will see a sign on your left pointing out the concessionary footpath which allows access to the fine ridge walk which crosses Chrome Hill – locally and appropriately known as the 'Dragon's Back'. Make sure you

Over the stile into Dowal Dale

Please note: time taken calculated according to the Naismith formula (see p.2)

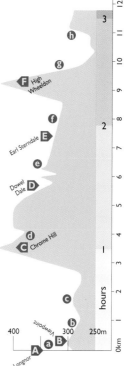

keep to the top of the ridge as the path is indistinct. Follow the ridge up the steep grassy slopes to a stile by a stately sycamore tree, with outstanding views back down the valley of the Dove and across the slightly lower, but no less impressively, pinnacled ridge of Parkhouse Hill, to which there is no access.

C Chrome Hill 071673

Chrome Hill (pronounced 'Croom' and with a 430m/1,411ft summit) is thought to have taken its unusual name from the Old English 'crumb' meaning 'curved' or 'sickle-shaped'. This is a perfect description of the curving ridge on which we are about to embark and which constitutes one of the finest ridge walks in the Peak District – an area not well-blessed with

Scabious on the lower slopes of Chrome Hill

such features. The Chrome Hill ridge, in Peak District terms, is sensational, weaving and dipping between limestone outcrops and small caves and arches and requiring a good head for heights if you stick to the actual crest all the way. The view from the summit is outstanding, extending as far as Axe Edge to the west and the dim outline of Kinder Scout beyond Buxton to the north.

d At the foot of the ridge a waymark points to a path which skirts a walled enclosure with Tor Rock upstanding to the right. Passing through an old wall and several stiles you reach a crossway. Turn right on the drive to Stoops Farms (signed Booth Farm) and walk to the junction with Dowel Dale road opposite High Edge. Turn right on this road which is fenced on the left, passing through Greensides and dropping down into the Dowel Dale by the pothole known as Owl Hole, on the left.

D   Dowel Dale 076678
The steep-sided defile known as Dowel Dale was formed, as explained above, as an undersea channel between coral reefs and although now dry except in its lower reaches, was once fed by a glacial meltwater stream which helped to carve out its steep sides and joined the Dove between Chrome and Parkhouse Hills. At the foot of the dale, in the cliffs opposite Dowall Hall, Dowel Cave has revealed evidence of Palaeolithic (Old Stone Age) occupation, perhaps 20,000 years ago, when it was used by hunting parties seeking game in the surrounding hills.

e At the head of Dowel Dale, just before it turns to head due south, take the stile on the left. The path beyond leads steeply uphill at first and then more easily, crossing a farm track and leading into another. Follow it down to the minor road near Harley Grange. Turn right and walk downhill, crossing the Longnor-Buxton road and into Earl Sterndale.

E   Earl Sterndale 090670
The grey, limestone cottages of Earl Sterndale may have family links with King's Sterndale, across the A515, but the 'Earl' is thought to derive from William de Ferrars, Earl of Derby, who held the estate in 1244. The village clusters around its small green, and is perhaps most famous for its welcoming pub with the unusual name of The Quiet Woman. Why she is quiet is obvious from the signboard – she has no head! The refurbished church of St. Michael's contains a 12th century font.

f   From Earl Sterndale, take the village street leading south-east, and then the minor road which branches off right past a small dewpond (locally 'mere') towards Abbotside Farm and the old quarry beneath Alderley Cliff. A National Trust sign opposite the quarry points to a stile and a path which ascends steeply up beside a drystone wall towards the conical summit of High Wheeldon. This is reached by a path coming up from Wheeldon Trees, on the left, passing the ruins of a lime kiln.

F   High Wheeldon 100661
The long ridged summit of High Wheeldon (422m/1,383ft) is one of the finest viewpoints in the White Peak taking in much of the route of the walk, and including the splendid peaks of the Upper Dove. Southwards, it extends to Longnor on its ridge and the Manifold Valley beyond and down the length of the Dove. Looking north-east, Longstone Edge above Bakewell can just be made out, as can Chelmorton Low and Eldon Hill, towards Castleton. Just below the summit to the north east is the locked entrance to Fox Hole Cave, where Palaeolithic and Neolithic remains have been discovered in a 54m/180ft long fissure-type chamber.

g   Turn south from the summit and walk steeply down to a drystone wall, turning right where it meets another and contouring down to meet the road to Crowdecote. If you don't want to climb the fence, there is a stile with a National Trust sign further along. Turn left onto the road and then right onto the unsurfaced, but walled, Green Lane which leads down to Beggar's Bridge across the River Dove.

h   From the bridge, the footpath crosses ancient ridge-and-furrow cultivations before climbing to a gate near a barn. Bear left for the final climb of the day, to reach Top o' th' Edge and a walled lane that leads back to the village street of Longnor. Turn right to regain the centre of the village.

View from Chrome Hill across to Parkhouse Hill

THOR'S CAVE FROM WETTON

START/FINISH:
Car park (with toilets) in
Wetton village. Infrequent bus
service and occasional Postbus
to Leek

DISTANCE:
9km/5½ miles

APPROXIMATE TIME:
3 hours

HIGHEST POINT:
Grindon, 316m/1,036ft

MAP:
OS Outdoor Leisure Sheet 24,
The White Peak

REFRESHMENTS:
Pubs in Wetton and Grindon,
café at Wetton Mill

ADVICE:
Some steep climbs in and out
of the Manifold Valley, but
nothing too strenuous. Special
care is required on descent
from Thor's Cave, particularly
when wet

WILDLIFE INTEREST:
Pipistrelle and Daubenton's
bats, fox, badger. Butterbur,
water crowfoot, marsh
marigold, harebell. Lapwing,
curlew, dipper, grey wagtail

Thor's Cave must be the archetypal caveman's home – a gaping 20m/60ft-high void in a crag 76m/250ft above the winding valley of the Manifold. Sure enough, firm evidence of prehistoric occupation has been found, and it has also attracted the attention of film-makers over the years. This walk dips in and out of the peaceful Manifold Valley, which never attracts the crowds of neighbouring Dovedale.

A Wetton 109553
Wetton is a typical nucleated White Peak village, attractively set around its tiny village green nearly 30m/1,000ft up on the limestone plateau and overlooking the deep valley of the Manifold. The Royal Oak public house welcomes walkers, and the parish church of St. Margaret's although severely re-built in 1820, retains its venerable 14th century tower.

a Start from the car park south of the village, turn right and then right again. At a 'T' junction turn left and take the lane on the left that is signposted 'To Thor's Cave'. Follow the upper drystone wall to a wall stile on the right which gives access to the cave around the foot of the crag to the right.

B Thor's Cave 098549
Care is needed to explore this stupendous void, because the bare rock floor slopes upwards from the entrance. The view, framed by the great dome of the entrance, across the winding

Manifold Valley towards Ossom's Hill is worth the visit alone. Formed from the harder reef limestones of the Carboniferous age, Thor's Cave may be the remnant of a much older cave system exposed by Ice Age glaciers. Further fissures lead on from the back of the cave, and other exist nearby where the Pleistocene and Romano-British remains have been discovered. The cave takes it name from the Norse god of thunder.

b Descend the steep steps which have been constructed through the trees from the cave entrance to the footbridge which crosses the River Manifold below. Take care when the ground is wet.

Inside Thor's Cave

C River Manifold 097551

The River Manifold exhibits that peculiarity of some limestone rivers in that for most of the year, it disappears to run in underground fissures. In the case of the Manifold, this happens at Wetton Mill and it bubbles to the surface again over 5km/3 miles downstream in the ground of Ilam Hall.

The valley is threaded by the Manifold Track, a walking and riding route converted by Staffordshire County Council as long ago as 1937 from the former trackbed of the Leek and Manifold Light Railway. The railway, which used Indian rolling stock, was a short-lived enterprise which opened in 1904 to serve the nearby copper mines at Ecton Hill, and closed in 1934. As a local person was heard to remark 'it starts from nowhere and finishes up at the same place'.

c Cross the Manifold Track to a stile and a footpath which contours up through Ladyside Wood, with splendid views back towards Thor's Cave. After leaving Ladyside Wood head towards Grindon Church Spire. A couple of stiles and a slab bridge across the stream leads you into Grindon village.

D Grindon 085544

The stately parish church of All Saints, Grindon – sometimes known as 'the Cathedral of the Staffordshire Moorlands' – is almost entirely Victorian, but it stands on a much more ancient site as the Saxon stone coffins and font inside testify. The graceful spire is a local landmark, seen in many views from the Manifold Valley. Note also in the church the plaque which records the air disaster during the bitter winter of 1947, when an RAF aircraft which was dropping food and supplies to the village which had been cut off by the snows, crashed on Grindon Moor. The 17th century Cavalier pub provides the social hub of this charming little upland village.

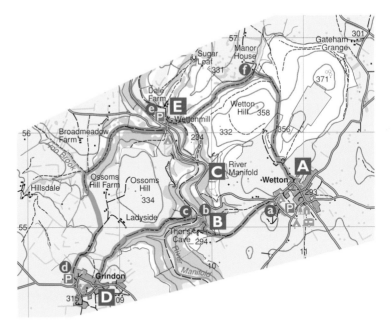

d From the car park near the church, turn right on the road, leaving it at a stile on the left near a gate just before the fork to Ossoms Hill. The path heads downhill through gates into the depths of the valley of the Hoo Brook, where you cross the footbridge and turn right following the edge of Ladyside Wood and contouring round Ossoms Hill. The valley known as Waterslacks leads down back into the Manifold Valley to Wetton Mill .

View across to Wetton Hill from Thor's Cave

View down the Manifold Valley

Please note: time taken calculated according to the Naismith formula (see p.2)

E Wetton Mill 095561

Wetton Mill is an attractive group of buildings grouped around Wetton Mill Bridge, which was rebuilt by the Duke of Devonshire in 1807 to serve his copper mining interests at Ecton Hill further upstream. The mill itself was a grist mill used by local farmers until 1857, when it closed down. All this area is part of the National Trust's South Peak Estate, and it was the Trust which provided the café and toilet facilities at the car park at Wetton Mill. The crag of Nan Tor, above the café, has caves which have revealed evidence of use by Mesolithic hunter-gatherers 8,500 years ago.

e From the café take the path which leads behind the mill, steeply uphill through a rock cutting and out into a lovely little dry valley. Bear left down into the valley and around the base of Wetton Hill to reach the former Pepper Inn, built in the late 18th century as an ale house, and later used as a smallpox isolation hospital and button factory.

f At a lane turn right at a stile crossing a footbridge and follow a wall which rises over the shoulder of tumulus-topped Wetton Hill. On entering the first field, bear left over a stile. You then pass through a former quarry site to enter the lane which leads you back into Wetton at Manor Farm, near the church. In Wetton turn left past the church and pub, and then turn right to reach the car park.

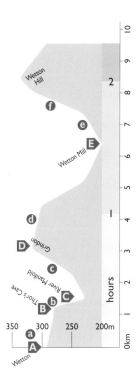

THE ROYSTONE GRANGE TRAIL

START/FINISH:
Minninglow Car Park on the
High Peak Trail, 800m/½ mile
south of Pikehall on the A5012
Cromford to Newhaven road

DISTANCE:
6km/4 miles

APPROXIMATE TIME:
Allow at least 2 hours

HIGHEST POINT:
On the High Peak Trail near
Gallowlow Lane, 330m/
1,082ft

MAP:
OS Outdoor Leisure Sheet 24,
White Peak

REFRESHMENTS:
None on route although there
is a pub in Parwich 3–5km/2–3
miles off the route

ADVICE:
A dry, former railway track,
followed by field paths which
can be muddy, and country
lanes

WILDLIFE INTEREST:
Lapwing, curlew, wheatear,
meadow pipit, skylark. Fox,
badger, weasel, stoat.

This is a journey back through over 6,000 years of Peak District history on a way-marked trail developed by the National Park Authority as a way of interpreting the fascinating history of a typical White Peak valley. A 10-year archaeological project by Sheffield University resulted in a wealth of knowledge being gathered about the history of Roystone Grange, and this easy walk visits all the sites of interest on its journey into the past.

A   The High Peak Trail, Minninglow Car Park 194582
The High Peak Trail follows the line of the former Cromford and High Peak Railway, which astonishingly was originally designed as a canal – the stations were called wharves – to link the Cromford Canal with the Peak Forest Canal at Whaley Bridge. Completed in 1830, it was one of the earliest operational lines in Britain, and when it first started the coaches and freight wagons were hauled by horses. Later locomotives were used, but stationary steam engines still had to pull the wagons up the steeper inclines, like that at Middleton Top, near Cromford. Among its unusual features was the Gotham Curve, about 1.6km/1 mile north from the Minninglow car park, where the line makes an 80° turn – the tightest on any British railway line. Now closed the line has been converted to the popular walking and riding route known to thousands of visitors today.

a   Set off south down the Trail towards High Peak Junction, passing through a rocky cutting and then over an impressive stone-built embankment on a sweeping curve with superb views. Ahead can be seen the spindly crown of beeches which marks the site of the Minninglow Neolithic Chambered Tomb. Continue on the High Peak Trail for over 1.6km/1 mile.

b Just past the junction (right) with Minninglow Lane, you pass the remains on your right of a 19th century brick kiln.

B   The Brick Works 205572
This partly-excavated Victorian brick-kiln complex manufactured refractory bricks for use in Sheffield's steel industry. The bricks were made from local deposits of high-

View towards Minninglow from the High Peak Trail

firing silica sands found in the pits near Minninglow Grange, in the valley below. Two kilns and the outlines of storage yards can be seen by the side of the railway by which the finished bricks were transported. They were used to build steel furnaces in places like the fast-growing city of Sheffield, and this industry was continued until quite recently at the Friden works near Newhaven, whose chimneys can be seen on the horizon.

c   Before the brick kiln a gate leads left onto Gallowlow Lane, where you get good views of the Minninglow tomb on the hilltop to the left (no public access).

C   The Minninglow Tomb
Enclosed by a spindly collection of ancient beeches and now surrounded by a moat-like plantation of modern conifers, the Minninglow Neolithic Chambered Tomb is one of the earliest prehistoric monuments in the Peak District.

The megalithic tomb was constructed on the summit of the 372m/1,220ft Minninglow Hill between 4,500 and 2,000 BC by Neolithic people who obviously appreciated the outstanding views from its windswept summit. At least four chambers were constructed from large blocks of limestone which were then covered by a massive circular mound of earth which has long since disappeared. The bones of the dead were buried in the chambers, and possibly taken out again on ceremonial occasions.

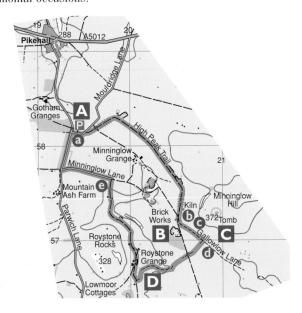

Abundance of flowers along the High Peak Trail

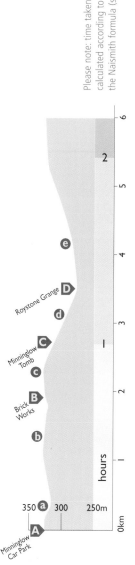

Like most of the prominent burial mounds in the Peak District, Minninglow was excavated by Thomas Bateman, the Victorian antiquarian, but even by his day, most of the prehistoric material had been plundered. He did, however find Roman coins and pieces of Romano-British pottery on the summit, showing that it may have been used by picnickers from the Romano-British farm in the valley below. The tomb site has since been restored and filled in by modern archaeologists.

d　After a few hundred yards on Gallowlow turn right at the footpath sign downhill and over a stile on a path which leads beneath the former railway and down through another stile into the Roystone Grange valley. Follow the wall on the left over a stile on the left and continue downhill with the wall now on your right. Go through the next stile into a field and bear left across the field to a track. Turn right into the farmyard of Roystone Grange.

D　Roystone Grange 201568
The award-winning Roystone Grange dig by Sheffield University has revealed the continuous use of this remote

little dry valley since Roman times. It has been established that some of the drystone walls still in use today were actually first laid down in Roman times, and are marked by the massive 'orthostat' stones in their base. The foundations of the medieval grange of Roystone – an outlying farm belonging to the Cistercian Abbey of Garendon in far-off Leicestershire – were discovered in the fields behind the prominent, chapel-like pump house building in the valley. In the field next to the pump house are the foundations of what could have been a Romano-British sheep pen, a matter of yards from where the modern farmer at Roystone erects his galvanised iron sheep pens for the annual shearing nearly 2,000 years later.

Below the pump house, on the hillside to the left of the track which leads down the dry valley to Ballidon Quarry, six low banks reveal a Romano-British field system. The main

Parwich

Romano-British farmstead and manor has been identified behind the now-disused dairy. This was occupied during the 2nd century by a community of British people who had been 'Romanised' after 300 years of Empirical rule, and who farmed the valley growing their crops and raising their livestock in this quiet White Peak backwater. These are the same people who may have enjoyed that picnic on the breezy summit of Minninglow.

e Walk through the farmyard of modern Roystone Grange, noting the fine barn on the left, and follow the lane which leads past the farm cottages to the junction with Minninglow Lane. Turn left here and follow the lane for about 800m/½ mile and at the junction with Parwich Lane, turn right and walk back along the lane to the car park, which is 400m/438 yards on the right.

THE RAILWAY TRAILS AND ARBOR LOW

START/FINISH:
Parsley Hay Car Park just off the A515 near Hartington. Buses between Bakewell and Buxton, and between Leek and Bakewell on Mondays and summer Sundays

DISTANCE:
11km/7 miles

APPROXIMATE TIME:
3 hours

HIGHEST POINT:
Arbor Low 374m/1,230ft

MAP:
OS Outdoor Leisure Sheet 24, White Peak

REFRESHMENTS:
At the Parsley Hay Cycle Hire Centre, or there is usually an ice cream van at the Hartington Old Signal Box on summer weekends. Also available at the campsite on the High Peak Trail just before Friden

ADVICE:
This is an easy half-day walk which sticks mainly to easily-graded former track beds of old railways, so no steep climbs, either. Take care on the busy A515

WILDLIFE INTEREST:
Skylark, meadow pipit, lapwing, curlew. Frog, great crested newt, dragonfly. Harebells, ox-eye daisy, birds-foot trefoil

The conversion of the former Cromford and High Peak Railway and the Ashbourne to Buxton Railway lines into what are now the High Peak and Tissington Trails was a typically innovative scheme by the pioneering Peak District National Park Authority in its early days. This easy walk samples both, with a diversion to the most impressive prehistoric site in the Peak – Arbor Low.

A   Parsley Hay 147636
The charmingly-named Parsley Hay, now a popular National Park cycle hire centre and picnic area, stands close to the junction of the High Peak and Tissington Trails. Originally known as the Parsley Hay Wharf (the Cromford and High Peak line was originally designed as a canal), it is now the hub of the trail-users and convenient for the exploration of both lines.

The Cromford and High Peak Railway was built at the start of the 'Golden Age' of railway building. Designed by Josias Jessop and opened in 1830, it was later taken over by the London and North Western Railway but fell under the Beeching axe in 1967. The Ashbourne-Buxton line was much more short-lived, opening in 1899 and closing within months of the High Peak line in September, 1967.

Ancient stone at Arbor Low

Cycling near Parsley Hay

Both lines were purchased by the National Park authority and Derbyshire County Council in the late 1960s, and converted into the popular walking and riding routes which they are today. But, as we will see, there are still many reminders of the past along the way.

a   Leave Parsley Hay and turn left, heading south to the fork where the High Peak Trail joins the Tissington Trail. Bear left onto the High Peak Trail, which shortly enters a deep cutting and passes under the A515 by the Newhaven Tunnel.

B   Newhaven Tunnel 151630

This 47m/51 yard long tunnel is an oddity in such an exposed place over 300m/1,000ft above the sea. Note the plaques above the entrance portals at either end. The northern portal pays tribute to the engineer and to the solicitor of the company 'Jos. Jessop Esq. Engineer' and 'Wm. Brittlebank Esq', while the one above the southern portal shows an originally horse-drawn railway wagon with the words 'Cromford and Highpeak Railway, 1825' surrounding it. Note also the heather growing on the cutting sides – a rarity in limestone country. Shortly after leaving the Newhaven Tunnel, the trail passes through the Derbyshire Wildlife Trust's Blake Moor nature reserve, an area of wetlands and flooded claypits away to the left, which is important for amphibians and other aquatic wildlife.

b   It is now straight ahead on the pleasantly-winding High Peak Trail for about 3.2km/2 miles to the former brick works at Friden Grange.

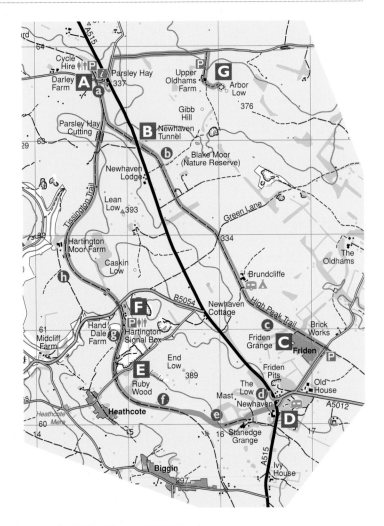

C   Friden Grange 171608

The now disused brickworks at Friden Grange once made heat-resistant refractory bricks for the furnaces and ovens used in the steel-making process. Its site here is explained by the fact that local pits were the source of high-grade silica sand which is needed in the manufacture of this type of bricks. The brickworks closed in the 1980s.

c   On leaving the trail at Friden walk out of the car park and turn left at the road. Turn right at the end of this road and left at the grassy triangle to reach the A515. Cross the busy A515 and walk past the derelict Newhaven Hotel.

Tissington Trail towards Parsley Hay

Please note: time taken calculated according to the Naismith formula (see p.2)

D Newhaven House Hotel 162601

This former coaching inn on the busy Ashbourne-Buxton turnpike once had stabling for as many as 100 horses. It was built by the Duke of Devonshire around 1800 on this once-profitable route, but is now is a sad state of disrepair and is a fine old listed building desperately seeking a new use.

d   At the far end of the hotel buildings, take the gate which leads up a field to a stile, and then follow this path through a series of stiles which lead past Stanedge Grange on the left. If you want to avoid the cows on this stretch of the route walk

Hartington Old Signal Box

down the A515 and just past Ivy House on the left turn right on the road to Biggin and pick up the Tissington Trail there.

e A gap leads through the shelter belt known as the Horseshoe Plantation, from where you drop down to the Tissington Trail, which runs across the foreground of the view, by bearing right through two squeezer stiles.

f You are now back on the Tissington Trail, where you turn north (right) and follow this for about 5km/3 miles back to Parsley Hay, with increasingly fine view westwards over Hartington and towards the hills of Ecton and Wetton which stand above the winding Manifold Valley. After about 800m/½ mile, you pass the Ruby Wood Plantation on your right.

E   Ruby Wood Plantation 150603
The Ruby Wood Plantation and picnic site was planted in 1991 to mark the 40th anniversary of the Peak District National Park, and is a good example of how, with the proper management, healthy woodland can be encouraged to grow even on these bleak heights.

g It is only a few more steps, through another limestone cutting and past some old quarry workings, until you reach the Old Signal Box at Hartington.

F Hartington Old Signal Box 149610

This splendid old wooden signal box was one of the few buildings connected with the former railway line which was not demolished when it was converted to a leisure trail. Carefully restored in its original livery, it is open as a visitor centre on summer weekends, and children (of all ages!) can enjoy the thrill of operating the old signal levers in the box, while enjoying a grandstand view down Hand Dale towards Hartington. There is also a car park, picnic area and toilets.

h The trail leads on through cuttings and over embankments which give a grandstand view of Hartington Moor Farm down to the left, with Long Dale beyond. The deep 'V' of the Parsley Hay cutting now looms ahead. This is another of the Derbyshire Wildlife Trust's local nature reserves, important for its unique geological cross-section through the limestone strata. You are soon back to your starting point of Parsley Hay.

i If you wish to visit the outstanding prehistoric site of Arbor Low, (and it should not be missed) it is less than 1.6km/1 mile away, across the A515. Take the Youlgreave road after a few yards and follow this for about 800m/½ mile to the sign (right) which leads through Upper Oldhams Farm (fee) to the monument.

G Arbor Low 160633

The great Neolithic henge and stone circle of Arbor Low has been called 'the Stonehenge of the North', but its remote setting gives it much more of a sense of closeness with the prehistoric past than its Wiltshire counterpart.

The henge was constructed between 3,000 and 2,000 BC probably as the focus for communal religious or ritual ceremonies. The circle of stones, now all fallen, were added later, and later still during the Bronze Age, a circular burial mound was superimposed on the henge's eastern rim.

A couple of fields away to the south is the even earlier Gib Hill burial mound, which was originally built in Neolithic times as a long barrow, and later, like Arbor Low, had a Bronze Age barrow superimposed on it. The views from both monuments across the rolling limestone plateau are superb.

LATHKILL DALE FROM MONYASH

START/FINISH:
Car park in Chapel Street, Monyash. Buses from Buxton (but not on Sundays) and from Bakewell (Monday–Saturday)

DISTANCE:
7km/4½ miles

APPROXIMATE TIME:
Allow 2/3 hours

HIGHEST POINT:
Monyash, 270m/885ft

MAPS:
OS Landranger Sheet 119 (Buxton, Matlock and Dove Dale) and Outdoor Leisure Sheet 24 (White Peak)

REFRESHMENTS:
Tea room, shop, and Bulls Head public house in main village street

ADVICE:
Many squeezer stiles at start, then fairly easy dale walking with a rocky scramble towards the end

WILDLIFE INTEREST:
Dipper, kingfisher, grey wagtail, nuthatch, wheatear. Jacob's Ladder, thyme, rockrose. Northern brown argus, orange tip butterflies

The Lathkill is a dale with Jekyll and Hyde qualities. On the one hand, it is part of the Derbyshire Dales National Nature Reserve, famous for its clear-running limestone river, and on the other, although hard to believe today, it was the scene of intense industrial activity during the last century. This easy half-day stroll from Monyash takes you into the heart of the Lathkill and illustrates the two sides of the dale's character.

A   Monyash 149665

Monyash – the Old English name means 'many ash trees' – was granted its right to hold a market in 1340, and the ancient market cross still stands on the village green. The reason for its importance high on the fast-draining White Peak limestone plateau were its five 'meres' (clay-lined ponds), of which only Fere Mere now survives. In the 18th and 19th centuries, it became an important lead mining centre, when most of the inhabitants were engaged in the dual economies of farming and mining.

a   From the car park walk down to the village green, passing the Market Cross, and turn left past the 'Bulls Head' crossing the road to enter the churchyard.

B   St. Leonard's Church 151665

The elegant spire of St. Leonard's Church, Monyash, celebrates the 800th year of its founding this year (1998). Heavily restored in 1887, the building retains its Decorated style transepts, aisles and nave arcades, reflecting the tiny village's former importance as a market township.

b   A path leads south through the churchyard through a series of squeezer stiles and into a walled farm lane which you follow until it ends at Fern Dale, a small dry tributary of Lathkill Dale, which is crossed by three stiles. At a gate, you join another farm track which leads directly to One Ash Grange.

C   One Ash Grange 169653

The name 'grange' almost always indicates an outlying farmstead which in medieval times belonged to a monastery or abbey, and One Ash Grange is no exception. This compact little settlement perched on the brink of Cales Dale was once owned by Roche Abbey in South Yorkshire. It is now better known for its Peak National Park Camping Barn, which provides cheap and simple overnight accommodation for walkers.

c   Follow the track to the left of the Camping Barn to a stile at the end of the Dutch barn. The path now descends sharply into the rocky defile of Cales Dale, which is followed (left) beneath impending limestone crags to cross the Lathkill and reach Lathkill Dale by a wooden footbridge.

D   Disappearing river 174655

The River Lathkill exhibits that strange feature of streams which run for all or part of their course across Carboniferous limestone. In summer, when the water level is low, it can disappear completely to run its course underground. This situation has been exacerbated by the centuries of lead mining in the area, after large-scale drainage of the workings led to a significant lowering of the water table.

Further downstream from the junction with Cales Dale, the path alongside the Lathkill enters Palmerston Wood, where the ruins of Mandale Lead Mine can be visited. A Cornish

Monyash Church and village pond

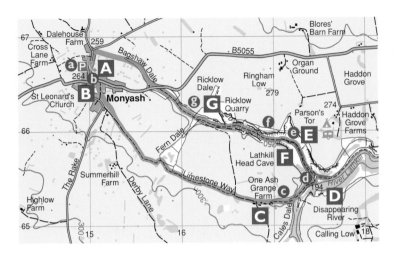

beam engine was used here to pump water out of the mine via a 10-m/33-ft diameter water wheel.

This part of the dale is probably the richest for wildlife, and you may see dipper and grey wagtail hunting in the clear waters of the river, and nuthatch and woodpeckers in the woodland. The more open dalesides are famous for their herb-rich flora where over 50 different species of plants have been identified per square metre. This is turn supports butterflies such as the orange-tip and northern brown argus.

d Turn left at the other side of the footbridge and walk up the path which leads westwards up the dale passing, after the first stile, the partly hidden adit to the Holmes Groove lead mine across the river to the left.

E Parson's Tor 172661
The bold limestone crag high up on the right, where another dry valley comes in from the right, is known as Parson's Tor. Known as Fox Tor until 1776, its name was changed to commemorate the tragic death of the Rev. Robert Lomas, rector of Monyash, who fell to his death from the tor when returning home from Bakewell on horseback one stormy night. He is buried in Monyash churchyard.

e Continue up the increasingly-impressive dale, now open and treeless. After a few more yards, to the left, the gaping maw of Lathkill Head Cave yawns.

Footbridge in Lathkill Dale

Please note: time taken calculated according to the Naismith formula (see p.2)

8

I¹/₂

7

g

6

Ricklow Quarry **G**

5

f

Lathkill Head Cave **F**

E **e**

Parson's Tor **e**

4

d

Disappearing River **D**

3

c

C

One Ash Grange

2

St Leonard's Church **b**

B 300   250   200m

a

A

Monyash

hours

I

0km

F Lathkill Head Cave 171659

Lathkill Head Cave is what is known as a 'resurgence' cave, and is where the River Lathkill emerges from the hillside in spectacular fashion during the winter months when the water level is high. Cavers have explored about 60m/200ft into the hillside, but this kind of activity is only for the experts, and non-cavers should not be tempted to enter too far.

f Continue up the dale, and where the limestone walls start to crowd in, in summer you may be lucky enough to see some fine stands of the rare Jacob's Ladder flowering in the dale bottom. The path is now confined to a rocky scramble, recently much improved after work by the British Trust for Conservation Volunteers, over and around some large boulders.

G Ricklow Quarry 164662

The scree of broken stones coming down from the right is from the now-disused Ricklow Quarry, from which 'figured marble' was won in Victorian times. This was a highly-fashionable polished grey limestone in which there were a large number of decorative crinoid (sea lily) fossils.

g The dale now opens up and you cross a series of stiles where in summer you may be ticked-off by the resident pair of wheatears, which nest in the broken down drystone walls in this part of the dale.

Eventually you emerge onto the B5055 Bakewell road by a stile. Turn left and cross the road to enter Bagshaw Dale, a shallow dry valley which is an extension of Lathkill Dale. Crossing a series of stiles and gates, you emerge through drystone walls onto the Taddington road, where you turn left into Chapel Street to return to the car park and village centre.

Looking south across to Cales Dale from above Lathkilldale

BRADFORD AND LATHKILL DALES

START/FINISH:
Youlgreave, reached by buses from Bakewell

DISTANCE:
About 6km/4 miles

APPROXIMATE TIME:
Allow two hours

HIGHEST POINT:
On Conksbury Lane, 267m/876ft

MAP:
OS Outdoor Leisure Sheet 24, The White Peak

REFRESHMENTS:
Café, shops and farmhouse teas in Youlgreave

ADVICE:
Easy riverside and field walking

WILDLIFE INTEREST:
Badger, dipper, grey wagtail, lapwing, heron. Harebell, meadow cranesbill, butterbur, trout, stoat, coot, moorhen, kingfisher

Youlgreave is a busy working White Peak village with what seems to be an everlasting parking problem. Its name is thought to be derived from the Old English for 'yellow grove' (a groove is the old name for a lead vein), and it was an important centre for lead mining for many centuries. It sits on a shelf of land between the Rivers Bradford and Lathkill, and this walk links the two, taking in the lower reaches of the Lathkill to where it joins the Bradford at Alport.

A   Youlgreave 210642

What's in a name? Although local people prefer the old spelling of 'Youlgreave', which is how it is pronounced, the Ordnance Survey insists on the extra 'e' for this limestone village, which also has the confusing local nickname of 'Pommy'. Youlgreave has the distinction of having its own water supply from the River Bradford, and its well-dressings, held in June, are centred on The Fountain, the water tank built in 1829 in the centre of the village. The parish church of All Saints has one of the finest Perpendicular towers in the county, and a wide, mainly Norman, nave in which the alabaster effigy tombs of the Cockayne family are particularly fine. The former Co-op is now the Youlgreave Youth Hostel and the boast is that men can sleep in a dormitory still labelled: 'Ladies Underwear'.

Bradford Dale

River Lathkill near Raper Lodge

a From the church walk up towards the 17th century mullioned Old Hall on the right and turn left down Holywell Lane, then after a few yards between houses to a squeezer stile which leads to a path down the bank of the River Bradford. Cross the footbridge to the opposite bank.

B   Bradford Dale 215642

Bradford Dale is among the less-heralded of the Derbyshire Dales. It is short but well sheltered by trees, and is the haunt of dipper and kingfisher. In its upper reaches, near Middleton-by-Youlgreave, Bradford Dale has some fine crags and caves where, during the Civil War, Sir Christopher Fullwood of that village was shot and killed as he hid from Parliamentary forces.

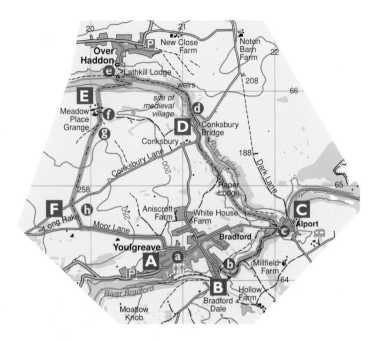

b Turn left after the footbridge and follow the riverside path, beneath the towering, tree-topped limestone cliff of Rheinstor. Cross the bridge to enter the hamlet of Alport.

C Alport 221646
This pretty little hamlet at the junction of the Bradford with the Lathkill is one of two Alports in the Peak District – the other one being a small community of farmsteads in the shadow of Bleaklow. Among Alport's fine old buildings are the old corn mill and the 17th century gable-fronted Monks Hall. The bridge built in 1718 replaced a ford.

c Cross the A524 Youlgreave road to a stile and a path which goes through a succession of stiles as it follows a fence above the River Lathkill, to the right. You cross the bridleway to Hodden Hall and then out onto another minor road just above Conksbury Bridge. Turn right here and down to the narrow Conksbury Bridge.

D Conksbury Bridge 212656
This is an ancient crossing place. The Old English name means 'Crane's' or Crannuc's fortified place', and the limestone hills surrounding this spot may have once held a hill fort dating from the Iron Age. The bridge dates from

The bridge at Alport

medieval times, it is first mentioned in 1269, and the remains of an extensive deserted medieval village have been traced in the fields above the river to the west.

d Follow the footpath along the river upstream from the bridge, now on the northern bank, passing a series of weirs in the river built to encourage the spawning of trout. A limestone crag now hangs over the opposite, heavily wooded bank. Through a series of stiles, you reach Lathkill Lodge and the entrance to the National Nature Reserve.

Please note: time taken calculated according to the Naismith formula (see p.2)

e Cross the river at Lathkill Lodge by the slab clapper bridge and ascend steeply up the hairpin farm track through Meadow Place Wood and out onto pastureland where two gates give access to the buildings of Meadow Place Grange.

E Meadow Place Grange 201658

The name 'grange' is usually the sign that the place was once an outlying farm of some medieval abbey, and Meadow Place Grange is no exception. The neat layout of the farm buildings around a central courtyard mark this as a classic grange site, in this case, associated with the Augustinian foundation of Leicester Abbey.

f Cross the courtyard leaving the barn on the right and climb up to the wall corner beyond the grange. There is a fine backward view of the layout of the grange from here, with the wooded gash of Lathkill Dale beyond.

g Take the diagonal path which can get very muddy that leads through stiles across three fields until the Conksbury Lane is reached. You cross the road from stile to stile or between facing stiles which lead to a path which crosses the end of the Long Rake lead vein.

F Long Rake 198647

In lead mining parlance, a 'rake' is a major lead vein where the ore is deposited between two vertical walls of rock. A rake such as Long Rake can run in a straight line for many miles across country, and they have usually been worked out by the old lead miners to a considerable depth underground, so can be potentially dangerous to explore. They are usually, as with Long Rake, planted with trees which keep livestock from grazing the lead-poisoned, or 'bellanded', ground around them. Long Rake, along with many other rakes, is still being worked to extract not the lead anymore but calcite and fluorspar, which are now much more valuable to the extractor.

h Continue on this path until it runs into Moor Lane. Turn left here and follow the lane back to your starting point in Youlgreave.

Lathkilldale showing path from Conksbury to Lathkill Lodge

MAGPIE MINE

START/FINISH:
Ashford-in-the-Water, served
by buses from Bakewell,
Buxton, and the Manchester-
Sheffield-Nottingham express
routes

DISTANCE:
10km/6 miles

APPROXIMATE TIME:
Allow 3–4 hours

HIGHEST POINT:
Near Magpie Mine c.
320m/1,050ft

MAPS:
OS Outdoor Leisure Sheet 24,
The White Peak

REFRESHMENTS:
Pubs in Ashford and Sheldon,
cafes in Ashford

ADVICE:
A steep, wooded climb out of
the Wye Valley and out of
Deep Dale, then easy field
paths

WILDLIFE INTEREST:
Redstart, dipper, grey wagtail,
wheatear. Fox, badger. Spring
sandwort, mountain pansy

There are few more evocative places in the Peak District
than the isolated and ghostly remains of the Magpie lead
mine, high on the limestone plateau near Sheldon. This is a
classic White Peak walk, starting from the charming village of
Ashford-in-the-Water (the 'water' being the River Wye) and
visiting Magpie Mine, undoubtedly the finest reminder of the
once-great lead industry of the Peak.

A   Ashford-in-the-Water 194696
There are plenty of clues as to how Ashford got its aristocratic
four-barrelled name. The 17th century Sheepwash Bridge
over the River Wye is a well-known landmark and probably
occupies the site of the original ford in this valley of ash trees.
Once a year, coinciding with the well-dressings, it is still used
for demonstrations of how sheep were washed before the
chemical dips of today. The church of Holy Trinity has a squat,
probably 13th century tower, and passing inside under the
Norman tympanum over the door, are several examples of the
once-prized Ashford 'black marble' – a type of polished grey
limestone – which was mined locally and became very popular
in Victorian times.

Ashford-in-the-Water

Ashford Church

a From the village centre, cross the river by the Sheepwash Bridge – noting the drystone pound where the sheep are collected prior to their immersion in the Wye. Carefully cross the busy A6 and turn right to the minor Kirk Dale road (look for signs marked 'Sheldon'). At the first sharp left-hand bend, take the path which leads off right alongside the river, eventually reaching the old bobbin mills beneath Great Shacklow Wood.

B The Ashford Bobbin Mills 182697

The partly-restored bobbins mills at Ashford (no access) were powered by the twin rusting iron water wheels still visible. They made bobbins from the local ash woods for the cotton mills at places like Litton and Cressbrook.

b The path now follows the old mill-race by the river to reach the entrance (left) to the impressive crater-like depression of Magpie Sough.

C Magpie Sough 179696

A sough (pronounced 'suff') is the Derbyshire word for an adit or tunnel built to drain a lead mine – as water in the mines was a constant problem for the lead miners of the 18th and 19th centuries. The 1.6km/ 1mile-long Magpie Sough, built to drain the famous lead mine we will be visiting later on this walk, took eight years to build and cost £18,000–35,000, a considerable sum of money for 1881 when the first water flowed through it, and a reflection of the importance placed on the task.

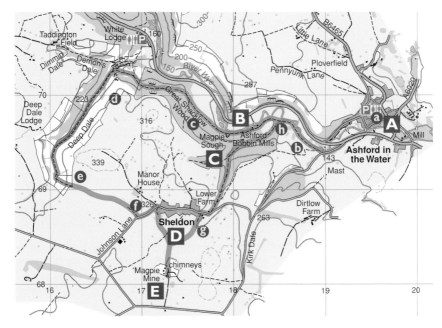

Magpie Sough became blocked when a shaft collapsed into it in the 1960s, and a tremendous volume of water built up behind the blockage. The result was a tremendous explosion of water in April, 1966 which swept away several hundred tons of shale and scree and partially blocked the River Wye. The sough was cleared and re-opened by members of the Peak District Mines Historical Society in 1974.

c The path now leaves the river and climbs steadily up through the mixed trees of Great Shacklow Wood before descending in open country again to reach the junction with Deep Dale coming down from the left by a prominent limestone crag. At this point, signs of an ancient settlement and prehistoric rock shelter have been investigated. Take care on the hillside particularly when leaving the wood.

d The next 1.6km/1 mile is an easy and gradual climb up the dry valley of Deep Dale (one of two which run into the Wye valley). Where the dale opens out, you enter a walled bridleway and turn left, and then left again by a stile to climb steeply up to the skyline.

e Bear left and follow a substantial wall, passing through several gates, eventually reaching a minor road just short of Sheldon. Turn left to enter the village.

D Sheldon 175688

Sheldon is a typical White Peak plateau village, with its limestone cottages standing back from its long village green and the simple little parish church of St. Michael and All Angels. Sheldon was first and foremost a mining community and Magpie Mine the main source of employment for many years. The interesting jump of 25 per cent in the village's population in the 1850s is explained by the employment of 14 lead miners from Cornwall, evidence of whose work we shall see later.

Winch at Magpie Mine

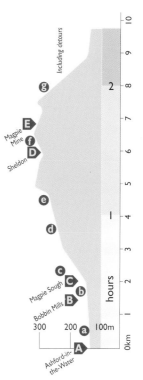

Please note: time taken calculated according to the Naismith formula (see p.2)

Including detours

g

E
Magpie
Mine
f
D
Sheldon

e

d

c
Magpie Sough C
b
Bobbin Mills B

300   200 a 100m

A
Ashford-in-
the-Water

hours

0km

Magpie Mine

f We follow in the footsteps of those lead miners by taking the squeezer stile on the right by the first house, heading through a series of stiles towards the buildings of Magpie Mine on the horizon.

E Magpie Mine 172682

Magpie Mine provides the most complete and interesting remains of a lead mine in the Peak. The mine was worked off and on from 1682 for about 300 years and has over 20 shafts in addition to the impressive remaining buildings which are in the care of the Peak District Mines Historical Society, which uses them as a field study centre. Chief among these are the Cornish Engine House of c1869, with its distinctive round Cornish chimney (Derbyshire miners were supposed not to have been able to construct round chimneys); the Agent's House of the 1840s, and the square 'Derbyshire' chimney alongside of the same period. The black-painted corrugated iron shed near the main shaft dates from the last unsuccessful efforts to win ore from the mine in the 1950s. All these buildings are now a protected ancient monument.

There were many disputes over the rights to the various lead veins which pass under Magpie Mine in the early 19th century, and these culminated in the 'violence on the mine' of 1833, when three miners were suffocated by sulphurous fires deliberately set underground by opposing miners. Interesting, no-one was successfully prosecuted for this act of violence, the conclusion being it was a case of six of one and half a dozen of the other.

Magpie is now a quiet and evocative spot, where you can find in early summer some of the best displays of lead-tolerant wildflowers such as 'leadwort', as the white flowered clumps of spring sandwort are known locally, and the yellow, purple and mixed 'faces' of mountain pansy on the lead spoil heaps. Summer visiting wheatears nest in the drystone walls around the mine buildings, and occasionally scold the visitor if he comes too close.

g Walk back to Sheldon by one of the many field paths used by the lead miners and turn right down the village street to Lower Farm on the left. Take the stile on the left just past the farm which descends towards Little Shacklow Wood.

h Bear right at a fork to take the higher path which contours above the wood on a fine promenade which drops gently down into the Wye valley again, with lovely views towards Ashford ahead. The path finally zig-zags down to the riverbank near the entrance to Kirk Dale (take care on the descent). Rejoin the outward path back into Ashford, across the A6.

Sheldon Church of St Michael

CHELMORTON, FIVE WELLS AND TADDINGTON

START/FINISH:
Chelmorton

DISTANCE:
10km/6 miles

APPROXIMATE TIME:
Allow 3–4 hours

HIGHEST POINT:
Sough Top 438m/1,437ft

MAP:
OS Outdoor Leisure Sheet 24,
The White Peak

REFRESHMENTS:
Pubs at Chelmorton, Flagg and
Taddington. Café at Taddington

ADVICE:
A breezy excursion on field
paths for most of the way. Be
wary of cattle in some sections

WILDLIFE INTEREST:
Lapwing, curlew. Common
lizard. Meadow cranesbill,
leadwort, mountain pansy

The Five Wells Neolithic Chambered Cairn is thought to be the highest such monument in the country, standing at over 430m/1,400 feet overlooking the Wye Valley near Taddington. This route follows a newly-opened concessionary path to the monument from the historic upland village of Chelmorton, returning via the village of Flagg, famous for its Easter point-to-point steeplechase races.

A   Chelmorton 113701
The 'fossilised' medieval strip fields of Chelmorton are famous in landscape history circles, and are best seen from the minor road dropping down from the Bakewell road at the end of this walk. The long lines of drystone walls which spread back either side of the village street perpetuate the strip fields of the farmers of 600 years ago. It is a familiar pattern in the White Peak, and can also be seen at Taddington and Flagg on this walk.

The charming name of the small stream which passes, mainly concealed, down the village street of Chelmorton is 'Illy Willy Water,' and the splendid little partly-Norman, 13th century church at the top of the village carries a locust weather vane on its spire to mark its dedication to St. John the Baptist. Chelmorton – locally-known as 'Chelly' – claims to be the highest village in Derbyshire, at over 365m/1,200ft.

a   From Church Lane, take the walled track which winds above the churchyard past the village spring along the line of an old lead rake, marked by various bumps and hollows, up the southern flank of Chelmorton Low (no access).

B   Chelmorton Low 114707
The fine escarpment of Chelmorton Low (446m/1,463ft) is crowned by a prominent pair of Bronze Age tumuli, where important tribal leaders were interred perhaps 4,000 years ago to watch over their successors. Like most of the Derbyshire 'lows,' the Chelmorton pair were excavated by Thomas Bateman of Middleton-by-Youlgreave during the 19th century.

b   Where the track crosses the Pilwell Gate bridleway, turn

Winter landscape near Chelmorton (Church Lane)

left up this walled lane until you reach the edge of the Five Wells escarpment, overlooking the A6. Here a sign leads right on the concessionary path beside a wall, to the Five Wells Chambered Cairn monument.

C   Five Wells Chambered Cairn 123711

All that is left of what was once a substantial, 21m/70ft diameter tomb are the two massive stone-built chambers which were once at its centre. The stones which once covered them were removed by wall builders about 200 years ago. There were two low entrances to the site, which when it was excavated in the 19th century, revealed the remains of 12 skeletons. Archaeologists now believe that the bones of the dead were taken from the tomb on regular, ceremonial occasions. Significantly, the Neolithic monument (built between 4,500 and 2,000 BC) commands extensive views over the valley of the River Wye to the north – another example of the ancestors watching over their land.

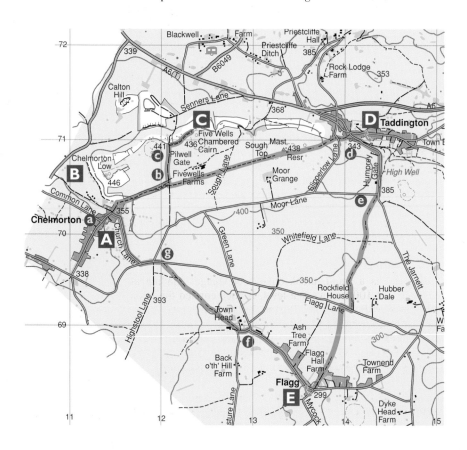

View northwards over Taddington

Please note: time taken calculated according to the Naismith formula (see p.2)

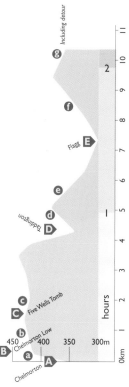

c   Retrace your steps back down the Pilwell Gate bridleway to where you joined it on the way up from Chelmorton. Turn left at the crossing point through a stile taking the path which leads below Fivewells Farm, shortly crossing Sough Lane on the ridge top which passes just below the high point of Sough Top (438m/1,437ft). The path now descends through a series of stiles to reach Taddington's main street. Follow the road into Taddington if you wish.

D   Taddington 142710

Taddington is a small, bleak one-street village standing at over 335m/1,100ft above sea level. It once carried the main road between Bakewell and Buxton, but is now thankfully by-passed by the roaring A6. The church of St. Michael at the western end of the village is notable for its gritstone tower and limestone walls and has what could be a Saxon cross shaft in the churchyard, from which are splendid views.

d   Back at the junction of the bridleway and the village street, ascend the lane known as Humphrey Gate, where

Chelmorton in evening light

again wonderful views can be enjoyed across the valley of the Wye and down to Fin Cop, above Monsal Head. Follow this lane past High Well, once the village's only source of water.

e At the road junction, go through the gate opposite, entering a shallow valley which is descended via a 'squeezer' stiles to pass Rockfield House and a minor road. Turn right then left to follow the line of the narrow, strip fields to reach Flagg through the farmyard of Flagg Hall to the road. Turn right into the village.

E   Flagg 135685

Flagg's unusual name probably comes from the Old Norse language, from a word that means 'the place where turfs were cut'. This typical White Peak plateau, linear village is perhaps best known for its point-to-point steeplechase races which are held every Easter weekend and attract large numbers of local people. The long strip fields lead off from the 'crofts' in the village street in typical fashion, and the northern end of the village is known as 'Town Head' which is again a typical White Peak name for the end of the village, found also as 'Townend' at Chelmorton.

f   At the end of the village street, turn left on a lane, and then right over a stile with Town Head Farm on you right towards another stile at the corner of a small wood. The path continues diagonally towards the north-west through more stiles to reach the Bakewell-Chelmorton road.

g   Turn left and follow the road across a cross-roads, taking the next right into Church Lane, which leads back into Chelmorton, now revealed ahead sheltering under the backing escarpment of Chelmorton Low. Note the pattern of strip fields mentioned in A. below you to the left, as you re-enter the village past the Church Inn.

Meadow cranesbill

CHATSWORTH FROM BAKEWELL

START/FINISH:
Car Park behind Old Market Hall National Park Visitor Centre, Bakewell. Regular bus services to Bakewell Square from Matlock, Chesterfield, Sheffield, Buxton, Nottingham and Derby

DISTANCE:
13km/8 miles

APPROXIMATE TIME:
Allow 4–5 hours, more if visiting Chatsworth

HIGHEST POINT:
Calton Pastures 289m/948ft

MAP:
OS Outdoor Leisure Sheet 24 (White Peak)

REFRESHMENTS:
Plenty of pubs and restaurants in Bakewell, restaurant at Chatsworth, tearooms at Edensor Post Office

ADVICE:
Can be muddy, especially through Manners Wood, but mostly easy going through pasture and woodland

WILDLIFE INTEREST:
Fallow and red deer, fox, badger, buzzard, skylark, lapwing, redstart, tawny owl. Sycamore, oak, foxglove, bluebells

Bakewell, strategically sited on a crossing of the River Wye, is the natural 'capital' and largest town within the Peak District National Park. This walk takes to the hills east of Bakewell to see the Duke of Devonshire's famous stately home of Chatsworth in its splendid setting in the neighbouring valley of the River Derwent, and returns over a landscape dotted with evidence of prehistoric settlement.

A   Bakewell 217685

Bakewell has recently undergone one of the biggest developments in its history, with the removal of the ancient Monday livestock market to a new Agricultural Centre across the River Wye. There has been a market in Bakewell for at least 1,000 years, but the right to hold the weekly market was granted in 1330, and it is still the major meeting and trading place for Peak District farmers, who also throng to the Bakewell Agricultural Show in August. Bakewell's ancient origins are reflected in the many Saxon stones in its hilltop parish church of All Saints, which also has two magnificent Saxon crosses in its sloping churchyard.

a   From the Old Market Hall turn right to cross the 14th century bridge over the Wye and then right again into Coombs Road. After 229m/250 yards turn left at a football sign opposite the entrance to the showground which leads up a track. Keeping the wall and later a hedge on your right, cross

Newly restored ceiling above the Great Staircase, Chatsworth House

Chatsworth Park

the bridge over the Monsal Trail, walk across the golf course and into Manners Wood. This section is steep. Follow the track and stream which leads steeply up through the wood to a ladder stile and out onto Calton Pastures. The path leads up past a pond and on to New Piece Plantation. Cross the stile into the plantation and on to another stile with a grandstand view of Chatsworth House and Park. To the left is the planned village of Edensor, which you now drop down to across the parkland.

B   Edensor 251699

The estate village of Edensor (pronounced 'Ensor') was created by the 6th Duke of Devonshire between 1838 and 1842, allegedly because the original village spoilt his view from the house. It is said that no two houses are to the same design, and that the Duke chose one of each from an architectural pattern book. The splendidly-proportioned parish church, built in 1867 by Sir George Gilbert Scott, houses many memorials to the ruling Cavendish family. There are more Devonshire family tombs in the churchyard, but

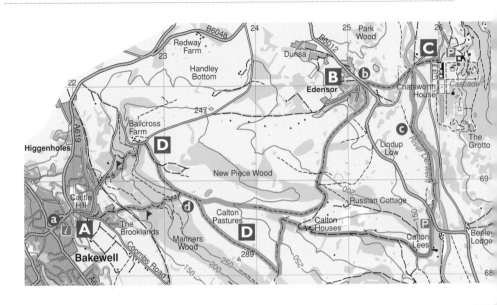

don't miss the simple marble slab to Kathleen Kennedy, sister of President John Kennedy and the widow of the Marquis of Hartington, who was killed in an aircraft crash.

b From the village cross the road and take the path opposite to reach the bridge over the River Derwent.

C Chatsworth House 261703 (OPEN MARCH–OCTOBER)
Be prepared for queues if you decide to visit the house, because Chatsworth, the Derbyshire home of the Duke and Duchess of Devonshire, is one of Britain's most-visited stately homes. The present house was built in the then-fashionable Palladian style by the 4th Earl of Devonshire between 1678 and 1707, but it stands on the site of a much-earlier Tudor mansion built by the legendary Bess of Hardwick, of which only the Hunting Tower now remains in the Stand Woods behind the house. There is also a popular Children's Farmyard and Adventure Playground in the woods behind the house, where walks lead up to the lakes which feed the spectacular Emperor Fountain in the immaculate gardens of the house.

Inside, Chatsworth is a vast treasure house of works of art collected from all over the world by successive Dukes, and highlights include the recently-restored magnificent painted ceiling in the Entrance Hall, and the wonderful collection of sculptures in the Sculpture Gallery.

The grounds of Chatsworth were landscaped by Lancelot 'Capability' Brown in the 1760s, who altered the course of the River Derwent and was responsible for planting the many fine trees which grace the parkland, and where herds of both red and fallow deer can be seen peacefully grazing today.

c At the bridge cross the road and walk downstream to the ruins of an old water mill. Turn right up to the road, cross it and turn left to walk past Chatsworth Garden Centre for about 1.6km/1 mile to Calton Houses. Follow the bridleway through a gate onto Calton Pastures, turn left alongside a wall, over a stile and up over open pasture to a ladder stile on the edge of Manners Wood. Make a sharp right turn before the ladder stile and continue along the footpath for 1.2km/¾ mile to reach the pond passed on the outward journey.

D Calton Pastures and Ball Cross 228691
The open grasslands of Calton Pastures are dotted with a series of Bronze Age tumuli, or burial mounds, which occupy

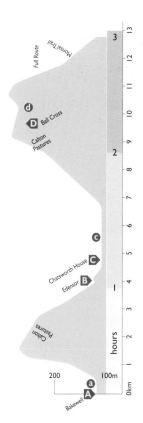

Please note: time taken calculated according to the Naismith formula (see p.2)

Edensor near Chatsworth

the high points of the ridge. It seems that the people who occupied this land up to 4,000 years ago venerated these high places, and used them to bury their leaders or most important people. In every case, these burial mounds have a distinctive crater in their tops, evidence of the work of Victorian archaeologists like Thomas Bateman of Middleton-by-Youlgreave, who systematically dug nearly all these tumuli and excavated the cremated remains of their occupants. Each tumulus still provides, however, the same sweeping views across to the Eastern Moors that our Bronze Age predecessors would have enjoyed. At the northern end of the pastures, fenced off with no public access, can be seen the embankments of the Ball Cross Iron Age hillfort, which

occupies a strategic promontory overlooking the valley of River Wye. This was never a fort in the military sense, but more likely a small fortified farmstead which may have been destroyed when the Romans arrived.

d You now have a choice of routes. You can either retrace your steps through Manners Wood and across the golf course back to Bakewell, or continue on the farm track past Ball Cross towards Ball Cross Farm, turning left on reaching a minor road and then left again down through the woods and back to the former Bakewell Station on the Monsal Trail. From here, it is a short step down Station Road and back across the bridge into Bakewell.

Pond on Calton Pastures

THE DALES OF THE WYE

START/FINISH:
Car park in front of the Monsal Head Hotel on the B6465. On the Bakewell-Tideswell bus route

DISTANCE:
11km/7 miles

APPROXIMATE TIME:
Allow 4 hours

HIGHEST POINT:
Near Bull Tor, 330m/1,083ft

MAP:
OS Outdoor Leisure Sheet 24, The White Peak

REFRESHMENTS:
Cafes at Monsal Head and Cressbrook. Pubs at Monsal Head and Taddington

ADVICE:
Easy dale walking, with a couple of steep climbs and descents. Flooding can make the approach to Cressbrook Mill impassable

WILDLIFE INTEREST:
Grey wagtail, dipper, redstart, heron. Yew, water crowfoot, watercress, bloody cranesbill, cowslip

Like many Derbyshire dales, the valley of the Wye changes its name every mile or so and is not actually known as Wye Dale until it approaches Buxton. But with every name change comes a change in scenery, and this easy circular stroll takes in some of the most beautiful sections through Monsal Dale, Miller's Dale and the delightfully-named Water-cum-Jolly Dale.

A   Monsal Head 185715
This is one of the most popular viewpoints in the most popular National Park, so arrive early if you want to find a parking spot! The view down two reaches of the River Wye is justifiably famous – looking north over Upper Dale towards Cressbrook and west across the famous Monsal Dale viaduct to the bold escarpment of Fin Cop, crowned by its Iron Age hill fort.

The construction of the Midland line – and the 24m-/80ft-high viaduct – in 1860 through this wonderful scenery prompted one of John Ruskin's fiercest outbursts in Fors Clavigera. There was a valley, he said, 'as divine as the Vale of Tempe' where the Gods could be seen 'walking in fair procession on the lawns of it, and to and fro among the pinnacles of its crags'. But now a railway had been 'enterprised' through it, and 'The valley is gone and the Gods with it, and now every fool in Buxton can be at Bakewell in half an hour and every fool in Bakewell at Buxton; which you think a lucrative process of exchange – you Fools everywhere'.

Rubicon Wall, Water-cum-Jolly

Monsal Dale weir, the River Wye

It is perhaps interesting to note that the Monsal Dale viaduct is now a protected and listed structure, and forms part of the Monsal Trail, a walking and riding route opened by the National Park in 1980. There are long-term plans by Peak Rail Ltd., to re-open this line for steam trains and passenger traffic.

a From the road which drops down into the dale, take the first path (left) signed 'Monsal Dale Weir' through the trees which runs above the viaduct, ignoring any paths leading off to the left. The path descends through the trees to meet the Wye beside a weir. A footbridge takes you to the northern bank, and you continue downstream. Through the trees opposite, the craggy landslip known as Hob's House is prominent, below the escarpment of Fin Cop.

B   Fin Cop hill fort 175710

Fin Cop is something of a rarity among the Peak District's Iron

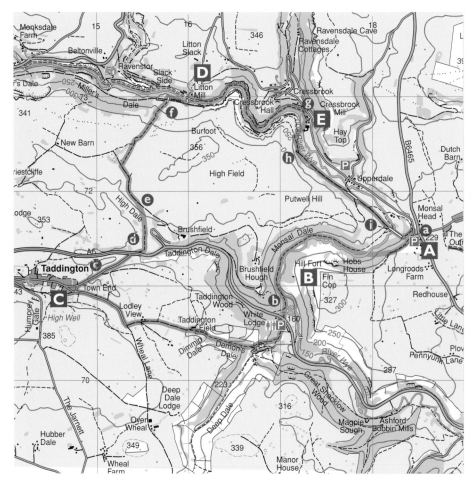

Age hill forts, being the only one so far positively identified on limestone. It is a large enclosure occupying the crest of the escarpment, and is heavily defended by an embankment to the south and east, utilising the natural defences of the steep gorge formed by the Wye on its northern and western sides. A recently-identified outwork to the east may have been used to corral stock in times of trouble, but no part of the site, to which there is no access, has ever been excavated.

b Just before you reach the A6, take the main path which leads to a stile at Lees Bottom and cross the road with care to the National Park's White Lodge car park. A stile leads off through the trees, and you bear right at a waymarker post to climb through rocky pastures above the mysterious little ravine known as Demon's Dale or Dell. The dry valley we follow to the right is the similarly-sounding Dimin Dale, and it leads up through trees to Taddington Field Farm. Enter the yard via a squeeze stile and through a gate to follow the drive from the farm westwards to Lodley View Farm, which leads on to the edge of Taddington at Town End.

C   Taddington 142710

Taddington is a typical one-street White Peak limestone

Cressbrook Mill

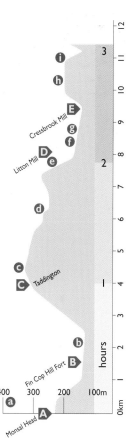

Water-cum-Jolly Dale, Miller's Dale

village, largely unspoilt and thankfully by-passed by the roaring traffic on the modern A6. The restored parish church of St. Michael and All Angels – at the far end of the village – has a slender spire rising from its 14th century tower and a 1,000-year-old Saxon cross shaft in its hilltop churchyard.

Older still, on Taddington Moor to the west of the village, is the Five Wells Chambered Cairn, which dates from the Neolithic, or New Stone, Age. Here in the highest monument of its kind in the Peak, the remains of the earliest settlers of the White Peak were buried, to watch over their successors from this airy vantage point.

c   From the east end of the village, take the lane which leads down to the A6 at the head of wooded Taddington Dale. Cross and take the bridleway which swings left then right to descend into steep-sided High Dale.

d   Turn left up this dry valley and where the wall stops, turn right following the path up a hollow to meet a walled lane with Bull Tor away to your left. There are good view from this high point to the hills beyond Castleton and as far as the long Kinder escarpment.

e   Turn left along the lane and then right through a stile and follow the path alongside a wall to another stile. Turn right to begin the long drop down into the Wye valley again at the Derbyshire Wildlife Trust's Priestcliffe Lees nature reserve. Descend through the scrubland to the Monsal Trail and Litton Mill, which is reached by a footbridge.

D   Litton Mill 160730

Litton Mill, currently awaiting conversion to a new life as holiday accommodation, began life as a cotton mill in the late 18th century, using the power of the River Wye. It was the scene, if the propagandist Memoirs of Robert Blincoe published in 1832 are to be believed, of some of the worst deprivations of child labour under the aegis of the cruel owner, Ellis Needham.

f   Follow the concessionary path past the mill and across the millrace by a footbridge and head downstream between the river and the mill cut. You will soon notice the impending limestone walls which mark the entrance Water-cum-Jolly Dale. This is a well-known climbing ground for the best of Peak District climbers, for whom features like the Cornice and Rubicon Wall, which overhang the path, hold no terrors.

Please note however that the dale is prone to flooding and can be impassable after heavy rain.

g The path now crosses the river again on a footbridge over a weir in a works yard, and then rises to the left to rejoin the Monsal Trail above the graceful buildings of Cressbrook Mill.

E Cressbrook Mill 173727

Cressbrook Mill is yet another example of a fine old building, originally built by Richard Arkwright, now urgently in need of a new use. It has faced dereliction for many years, but now has planning permission for re-use again for accommodation. The present Georgian-style building, with its fine cupula bell-tower which once called the apprentices to work, dates from 1815. But while Litton Mill, 1.6km/1 mile upstream, was notorious for the ill-treatment of its young employees, Cressbrook's owner, William Newton, is said to have treated his apprentices well.

h The last 1.6km/1 mile of the walk follows the Monsal Trail along its 'enterprised' embankments and cuttings above Upper Dale, passing the vestiges of the platform of what was once Monsal Dale Station.

i Soon, your starting point of Monsal Head appears ahead, and the final flourish of the walk is the crossing of that famous – or infamous – viaduct, with fine views up and down the valley. A path leads off to the left at the end of the viaduct and up through the trees to the starting point.

Monsal Dale after a freak blizzard

TIDESWELL AND CHEE DALE

START/FINISH:
There is a car park at Tideswell Dale 1.2km/¾ mile along the route. Buses from Sheffield Buxton and Bakewell call at Tideswell

DISTANCE:
10km/6 miles

APPROXIMATE TIME:
Allow 2–3 hours

HIGHEST POINT:
Wormhill, about 335m/ 1,100ft

MAPS:
OS Outdoor Leisure Sheet 24, The White Peak; Harveys Dark Peak South

REFRESHMENTS:
At Tideswell, Miller's Dale or Wormhill

ADVICE:
Mainly easy dale and trail walking

WILDLIFE INTEREST:
Ash, sycamore. Nottingham catchfly, bloody cranesbill, spring cinquefoil. Dipper, heron, redstart, chaffinch. Basalt outcrops are of geological interest

This easy 10km/6 mile walk explores the beautiful dales to the north of the River Wye from the 'cathedral town' of Tideswell, an historic settlement founded on the wealth won from wool and lead. En route it visits Monk's Dale, part of the Derbyshire Dales National Nature Reserve and the hilltop village of Wormhill, returning along the Monsal Trail via glorious Chee Dale.

A Tideswell 152755

Tideswell has the urbane air of a town twice its size, and this air of importance stems back to the mid-13th century, when it was granted the right to hold a weekly market. Street names like the Pot Market in the centre of the village recall its former bustle, but the most convincing proof of Tideswell's past glories is its magnificent parish church of St. John the Baptist. Known as 'the Cathedral of the Peak', this mainly 14th century church with its Perpendicular-style, pinnacled tower has a wonderfully light and airy chancel in the Decorated style and some of the finest monuments and brasses in the Peak. Tideswell's famous well-dressings, which take place in June, are among the most technically-accomplished in the area and attract large crowds.

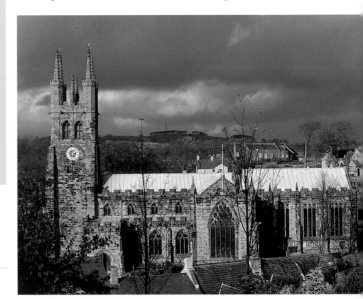

St John the Baptist's Church, Tideswell

Close-up of Tideswell well-dressing showing petals and seeds, 1998

a   From Tideswell, walk south on the B6049 which descends towards the Tideswell Dale car park and picnic area, which is reached through an avenue of stately beeches on your left.

B   Tideswell Dale 154742

Tideswell Dale was once the site of an ugly quarry where the black, igneous basalt which outcrops here was won for use in road-making. But an ambitious restoration scheme by the National Park Authority early in its history demolished the old quarry buildings and converted the dale into one of its first nature trails, best known for its geology, but also for its wealth of wildflowers, which here include orchids.

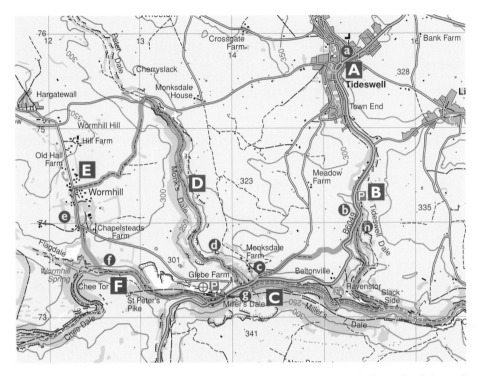

b Turn left out of the car park and walk down the dale road to the large 'S' bend, where you bear right across the layby and enter the fields by a squeezer stile. The path runs diagonally across several fields to reach a walled track which joins Meadow Lane, where you turn left and drop down to reach the road again at Miller's Dale.

Cheedale Viaduct

Climbing crag, Ravenstor, Miller's Dale

C   Miller's Dale 141733

The old station buildings at Miller's Dale were once the hub of one of the busiest junctions on the former Midland line, now the Monsal Trail. The double track and sidings were the junction for Buxton on the Midland line, and Miller's Dale was the introduction to the Peak District for many of those early tourists. The station opened in 1863 and 40 years later it was extended and a second viaduct built. The old station buildings are now used as a ranger briefing centre for the Monsal Trail.

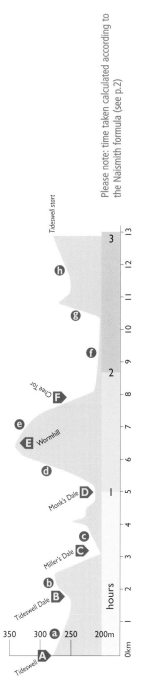

Please note: time taken calculated according to the Naismith formula (see p.2)

c   Walk down into the hamlet of Miller's Dale and turn right adjacent to St Ann's Church up an alleyway with steps. At the top go through a gate and turn right along a wall to descend into Monk's Dale, part of the Derbyshire Dales National Nature Reserve.

D   Monk's Dale 135740

Monk's Dale became part of the Derbyshire Dales NNR in 1972 and about 60 ha. is now protected. It is famous for its marvellous limestone-loving flora, such as the rare Nottingham catchfly, bloody cranesbill and spring cinquefoil. The woodlands of Monk's Dale are much younger than those of Lathkill or Dovedale, and consist mainly of ash and sycamore. But the ground flora in the woodland is exceptionally rich, with herb Paris, moschatel and dog's mercury abundant. The north-south running dale is normally dry during the summer months in its upper part where an occasional stream runs through in the winter. In the damper areas of the lower dale, where springs fed the stream, marsh marigold, brooklime and blue water speedwell thrive.

d   Walk up for a glorious 1.6km/1 mile through the steep-sided dale, crossing the stream at one point by a footbridge. The dale gets more heavily-wooded at its northern end, where you meet the former Tideswell Road and turn left, then left again through a stile (not signed) steeply up the field to reach a walled bridleway which leads to the hilltop hamlet of Wormhill. Please note slippery limestone can make Miller's Dale dangerous underfoot when wet.

E   Wormhill 123743

Perhaps Wormhill's most greatest claim to fame is that it was the home of James Brindley, the virtually illiterate pioneer of canal building, who was born at the nearby hamlet of Tunstead in 1716. There is a simple memorial on the village green to this genius of construction engineering who changed the face of Britain during the 18th century by his brilliant canal schemes. The first was the Duke of Bridgewater's canal between Worsley and Manchester, which was built between 1759–61, and included Britain's first aqueduct. Brindley died in 1772 at the age of 56.

e   Walk through the village, going down hill past the late 17th century Wormhill Hall on the left and just after passing Hassop Farm on your right, take the footpath signposted Chee Dale. This descends steeply past a number of springs into the dale, with the limestone buttresses of Chee Tor ahead.

Litton Mill village

F   Chee Tor 123733

Chee Tor is a 90m/300ft bastion of limestone with some demanding rock climbs on it. But on the tree-skirted peninsula above the crags, a well-developed Romano-British settlement site from the 3rd and 4th century AD has been identified. It is visible in aerial photographs as a series of lynchets and low stony banks which define several yards and house sites, with short lanes in between.

f   On reaching the riverside path, turn left keeping the river on your right and when you meet a road turn right down to the B6049 and left to pass under two impressive metal railway viaducts, which now carry the Monsal Trail. Please note this is a busy road with no footway.

g   Back at St. Ann's Church, Miller's Dale, bear right along the road signposted to Litton Mill, eventually turning sharply left (signposted) at the southern end of Tideswell Dale. The crag of Ravenstor stands out to your left, as you walk through the dale, noting the basaltic outcrops in the old quarry to the right.

h   After about 800m/½ mile, you re-emerge on the B6049 to walk back up the hill into Tideswell.

ELDON HOLE

START/FINISH:
Peak Forest, served by
Sheffield–Chapel-en-le-Frith
buses

DISTANCE:
About 6km/4 miles

APPROXIMATE TIME:
Allow 2 hours

HIGHEST POINT:
Back of Eldon Hill, near
Slitherstone Mine,
448m/1,470ft

MAPS:
OS Outdoor Leisure Sheet 24,
The White Peak and Sheet 1,
The Dark Peak. Harveys, Dark
Peak South

REFRESHMENTS:
Shop and pub in Peak Forest

ADVICE:
Field walking and through
pastures showing the remains
of lead mining. There may be
blasting in the quarry at Eldon
Hill

WILDLIFE INTEREST:
Bats, including pipistrelle and
noctule. Weasel, buzzard,
lapwing, curlew, stoat,
mountain pansy, leadwort,
kestrel, goldfinch

Eldon Hole – one of the original 'Wonders of the Peak' and long thought to be bottomless – is the objective of this easy, half-day walk on the northern edge of the White Peak. It starts from the village of Peak Forest whose name perpetuates the former medieval Royal Forest of the Peak, where kings and princes hunted quarry such as the 'conies', or rabbits, which are still remembered in the name of Conies Dale.

A Peak Forest 113792
The village of Peak Forest is bisected by the busy A623 Baslow-Chapel road, but its name gives away its history, just as Chapel-en-le-Frith does a few miles down the road. It was once part of the Royal Forest of the Peak (see below), and Chamber Farm, west of the village, is thought to have been the site of a Swainmote Court where offenders who broke the strict forest laws were dealt with by the Steward of the Forest and over 20 foresters.

Peak Forest's other claim to fame is its parish church, unusually dedicated to King Charles the Martyr and founded in 1657. By a quirk of ecclesiastical law, from 1665 until the passing of the Marriage Act in 1753, the minister here had the power to issue marriage licences, and many runaway marriages were performed, making Peak Forest the Peak's Gretna Green. One of these was to be the unfortunate Allan and Clara, who were murdered in The Winnats Pass at Castleton in 1758. Although not strictly legal, the custom survived despite the change in the law until around 1804.

Peak Forest towards Ox Low

Looking into Eldon Hole

B The Royal Forest of the Peak

The Royal Forest of the Peak was a 100km²/40 sq. mile area between the Rivers Wye and Etherow which was originally administered from Peveril Castle as a hunting ground. In many ways, it was an early example of the preservation of the area, where wild animals such as wolves, wild boar, wild cat and deer were protected so they could be hunted by visiting kings and princes. Edward I is recorded as staying at Tideswell, another hunting centre, for three days in 1275, and Henry I and II were also regular visitors.

a From the cross-roads (two adjacent T-junctions) in the village centre, go opposite the church north into Church Lane to the hamlet of Old Dam. At the road junction, turn left and then right at Eldon Lane End Farm into Eldon Lane. The lane becomes a track after Sweet Knoll Farm. Bear left after the stile and keep the wall on your left.

b Just past an old lead rake marked by a line of trees on your left, a path runs above the rake towards the open pothole of Eldon Hole where care should be taken. Note: there is no official access to Eldon Hole.

C Eldon Hole 116809

Long thought to be bottomless, Eldon Hole is the biggest open pot hole in the Peak. As one of the original Wonders of the

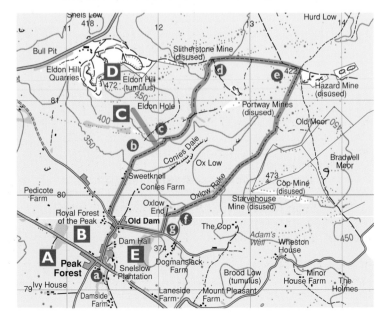

View from Eldon Hole looking
southwards

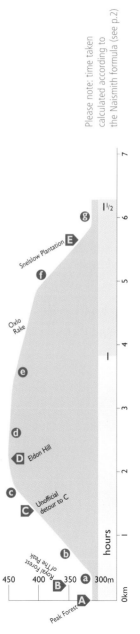

Please note: time taken
calculated according to
the Naismith formula (see p.2)

Peak, it was a place of fear and dread to local people. Tales of
people being lowered into it and coming back out as gibbering
idiots are legend. A goose which was sent down the fearsome
abyss is said to have emerged three days later at Peak Cavern
in Castleton, with its feathers singed, having been to Hell and
back. Charles Cotton, an author of the *Wonders*, claimed he
had let out 800 fathoms (1,463m/4,800ft) of line into it
without finding the bottom, but when it was eventually
descended in 1780, it was found to be only 76m/245ft deep,
with other chambers leading off. Daniel Defoe describes
Eldon Hole in his *Tour Through the Whole of Great Britain*.

c Return to the path that you left beyond Sweet Knoll Farm
and continue climbing over the eastern shoulder of Eldon Hill
to reach a gate onto a broad walled lane.

D   Eldon Hill 116812
Eldon Hill (no access) at 470m/1,543ft is one of the highest
limestone hills in the Peak District, and commands extensive

views towards the Mam Tor ridge and south across the White Peak plateau. Its name means 'elves hill' but today's elves are the quarrymen who have blasted away the whole of the western side of the hill in their quest for aggregate limestone. This ugly quarry has been dubbed 'the worst eyesore in the Peak' and the National Park Authority fought a 20-year battle to close it down, eventually succeeding in 1995, although processing of stone still continues on the site and there may be some blasting at the quarry face.

d Go right along the lane and continue eastwards through a landscape pitted and scarred by generations of lead miners. The descriptively-named Slitherstone Mine is on the hillside to your left.

e Just after the metalled lane leading left towards Rowter Farm, you turn right on the Limestone Way, following a wall south to a gate. Continue down the lane with Oxlow Rake on your right. The rounded hill to the right is Ox Low (430m/1,412ft) with the shallow, dry depression of Conies Dale beyond that. The limestone outcrops of Conies Dale are

typical of the open, uninhabited waste which was the Royal Forest of the Peak.

f   You then cross a farm track and take the stile in the wall opposite, veering left now to reach Old Dam Lane again. The tumulus-topped hill opposite is Snelslow, now clothed in a plantation.

E   Snelslow Plantation 119794

Despite its name, the area around Peak Forest is not noted for its trees, but those which are there add a vital softening touch to what could be a bleak landscape. Snelslow Plantation is a good example of sensitive woodland management by the National Park Authority. It thinned this exposed, hilltop wood and re-planted it in a scheme which won a Centre of Excellence award from the Forestry Authority. One enterprising young forester even managed to create a wooden sculpture in the middle of the plantation.

g   Turn right here to walk back to Church Lane turning left to re-enter Peak Forest and resume your outward route.

Towards Old Dam, Peak Forest

CASTLETON, CAVES AND CRAGS

C astleton lies on the great geological divide of the Peak District, at the northernmost extremity of the limestone White Peak where it dips under the shales and grits of the Dark Peak. This geology has provided its greatest attraction, and the series of show caverns attract huge numbers of visitors each year. But even if it didn't have the caves, the environs of Castleton would merit a visit, as this walk shows.

START/FINISH:
The Square, Castleton. Served by buses from Sheffield, Chesterfield and Bakewell

DISTANCE:
6km/4 miles

APPROXIMATE TIME:
Allow 2–3 hours

HIGHEST POINT:
Near Rowter Farm, 440m/1,444ft

MAPS:
OS Outdoor Leisure Sheet 1, The Dark Peak; Harveys, Dark Peak South

REFRESHMENTS:
Pubs and cafes in Castleton

ADVICE:
Mostly easy walking in dales and fields, with a short road section through the Winnats and quite hard climb up Cave Dale

WILDLIFE INTEREST:
Blue John, limestone fossils, pipistrelle and Daubenton's bats, skylark, meadow pipit, lapwing, curlew, wheatear

A Castleton 149830

The little township of Castleton was founded in the shadow of the imposing castle founded shortly after the Conquest by William Peveril, William of Normandy's son, on the naturally-defensive neck of land between the impressive gorge of Peak Cavern and Cave Dale. The present roofless keep dates from 1176, and was built by Henry II to oversee his prized Royal Forest of the Peak, a hunting preserve of medieval kings and princes. The planned town beneath never quite filled the confines of the still-visible Town Ditch, but the interesting medieval parish church of St. Edmund may originally have been the garrison church for the castle. Castleton is famous for its Garlanding Ceremony, held annually on Oak Apple Day (May 29), which is probably the remnant of a pagan ceremony welcoming the spring.

a   From the large village square, walk up Bargate and take the concealed entrance to Cave Dale (this should be signposted Limestone Way) and pass through a stile into the dale.

Castleton Cross and Youth Hostel

Cavedale, Castleton

B   Cave Dale 150825

The steep-sided confines of Cave Dale, once thought to be a collapsed cave system are now thought to have been carved out by the rushing meltwaters of an Ice Age glacier. Whatever caused its creation, the result is spectacular – a craggy, dry-bottomed limestone canyon watched over, to the right, by the impregnable keep of Peveril's Castle. Several caves lead off from beneath the crags of Cave Dale, and beneath your feet as you walk up the dale is the ever-dripping cavern of Roger Rain's House in Peak Cavern.

b   As the dale path gets steeper, with ever-expanding views back to Peveril Castle and the cone of Win Hill in the background, it narrows again through gates and stiles to a short gated road at the junction with the Dirtlow Rake bridleway. Turn right here over a stile and then a second one (right) which leads onto Rowter Lane.

c   Rowter Lane is followed for about 1.6km/1 mile, passing the farm of the same name over to the right, with the great

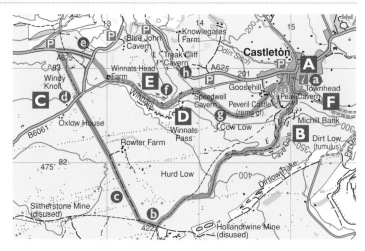

bulk of Mam Tor filling the skyline ahead. Note in the meadows over to the left, the distinctive bumps and hollows left by old lead mine workings. Several abandoned mine shafts are found here, and on the grassed-over waste hillocks, the beautiful, lead-tolerant purple and yellow flowers of the mountain pansy can be seen in summer.

d   Reaching the B6061, go straight ahead over a stile on a grassy track to reach the abandoned quarry and gaping, low cave entrance of Windy Knoll (National Trust).

C   Windy Knoll 126831

The Windy Knoll Cave and Quarry is one of the classic sites in Peak District geology and prehistory. On excavation, the impressive low cave was found to be the Ice Age den of brown bear, wolf and hyena, which preyed on the mammoth, woolly rhinoceros, reindeer, ox and red deer grazing the Arctic tundra outside. Although no remains have been found, it is hard to believe that Stone Age man did not also use the inviting shelter provided by the cave. And outcropping in the small quarry above has been found quantities of the rare mineral, elaterite, a sticky, tarry substance more commonly found today in the 'tar lakes' of the Caribbean.

Winnats Pass

e   Continue down to meet the A625 and turn right and right again at the junction beneath the crumbling face of Mam Tor, with fine views down the Hope Valley ahead. A stile leads left across the fields around the back of Winnats Head Farm, which stands at the head of the impressive canyon of the Winnats Pass (National Trust).

D The Winnats Pass 135826

Surely one of the wonders of the Peak, the Winnats (the name means 'wind gates') has now regained its status as the main entrance to Castleton and the Hope Valley from the west, since the collapse of the Mam Tor road in 1977. The steep 1:5 gradient must have made it an exciting ride by coach and four, but it remains one of the most thrilling motor roads in the Peak. The Winnats was the scene of the infamous murder of Alan and Clara, two runaway lovers, in 1758.

The old theory that it was formed from a collapsed cave system is now discounted. Modern geologists now believe that the craggy canyon was formed 350 million years ago as an undersea channel through the coral reefs of the Carboniferous period.

f Walking down the Winnats is by far the best way to appreciate the soaring rock architecture of this superb little canyon which cuts through the reef limestones of Treak Cliff, which extends away to the left.

E Treak Cliff 135831

Treak Cliff, with its famous caverns of Treak Cliff and Blue John, is said to be the only place in the world where the semi-precious mineral known as Blue John, is found. A purple, blue, white and yellow banded flourspar, Blue John was formed by hydrocarbons being forced under great pressure into cavities in the limestone where it crystallised. It is said

Entrance to Winnats Pass and Speedwell Cavern from the path below Cow Low

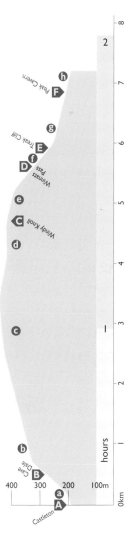

Please note: time taken calculated according to the Naismith formula (see p.2)

Field patterns leading to
Winnats Pass

to have got its name from the French 'Bleu et Jaune' – blue
and yellow – and it is now worked into a range of bowls and
ornaments by a skilled process which involves the brittle
mineral being impregnated with resin.

Another of Castleton's show caves, the Speedwell Mine, a
former lead mine reached by an underground canal boat trip,
is at the foot of the Winnats on the right.

g A gate leads off to the right just past the Speedwell Cavern
and this path leads across the face of Long Cliff below Cow
Low to enter Castleton again at Goosehill Bridge. It is a short
step from here to visit Peak Cavern, following the footpath
alongside Peakshole Water to the right.

F   Peak Cavern 149826

One of the original Seven Wonders of the Peak, Peak Cavern was long thought to be an entrance to Hell. In ancient times it was known as 'the Devil's Arse' and the river which flows through it is still known by cavers as the Styx. Peak Cavern has the largest cave entrance in Britain, and for 400 years a small community of rope-makers lived within its gaping maw in 'a village which never saw the sun'. Remains of their rope making equipment, and the smoke from their cottages which blackened the cave ceiling, can still be seen.

h   From Peak Cavern, turn right to return to the Market Square and the village centre.

Mist rising around Peveril Castle and Mam Tor

STANTON MOOR

START/FINISH:
Winster, served by occasional buses from Bakewell

DISTANCE:
10km/6½ miles

APPROXIMATE TIME:
Allow 3–4 hours

HIGHEST POINT:
Stanton Moor 323m/1,060ft

MAP:
OS Outdoor Leisure Sheet 24, The White Peak

REFRESHMENTS:
Pubs at Winster and Birchover

ADVICE:
Field and lane walking, with a little moorland stroll

WILDLIFE INTEREST:
Heather (Stanton Moor), meadow pipit, lapwing, curlew. Fox, badger, brown hare

Stanton Moor has always been a place apart, a little island of Dark Peak gritstone moorland almost completely surrounded by the limestone White Peak. This 'lost world' isolation must have made it important to prehistoric man, because during the Bronze Age it became a focus of ritual and burial activities, and over 70 tumuli have been identified amongst the rank heather.

Cork Stone, Stanton Moor

A   Winster 241605

The arcaded 17th century Old Market Hall in Winster was the first property to be acquired by the National Trust in the Peak District (in 1906), and is open at summer weekends. It gives a clue to the former importance of Winster, whose wealth was founded on the abundant lead mining remains to be found in and around the village. Other evidence of Winster's past importance are the imposing Georgian Winster Hall, now a public house, and the Miner's Standard public house on the village outskirts, which refers to the standard measure used to weigh lead ore. Winster is also famous for its Pancake Day races held on Shrove Tuesday every year.

a   From the Old Market Hall, follow Woodhouse Lane northwards signposted Birchover and at a gate go left through a stile downhill into the valley of the Millclose Brook. This is crossed and the route then rises through stiles and gates through a landscape littered with lead mining remains to the walled Clough Lane.

b   Cross Clough Lane by facing stiles and make for Barn Farm, on the outskirts of Birchover, which is away to your left. Turn right before reaching the farm at a signpost, on a path which leads around the head of the wooded clough of Sabine Hay Wood, down to your right.

c   Turn left on reaching a minor road, then follow a track right which leads onto the bracken covered slopes of Stanton Moor.

Nine Ladies Stone Circle, Stanton Moor

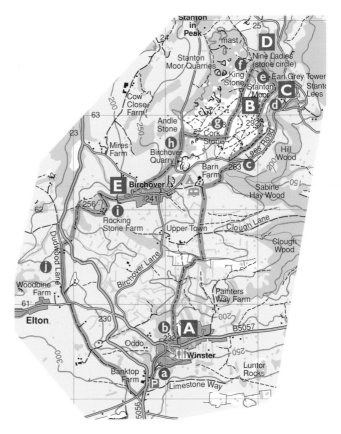

B   Stanton Moor 245630

Historian H.J. Massingham described Stanton Moor as 'as thick with tumuli as a plumduff with raisins', and at least 70 of these burial mounds have been identified, along with ring cairns and stone circles, including the most famous Nine Ladies Stone Circle and its associated outlying King Stone (see below).

Most of the evidence for Stanton Moor's prehistoric past was uncovered by the father and son team of J.C. and J.P. Heathcote of Birchover, where they kept a museum of their carefully-recorded finds in the old village Post Office for many years. All the finds are now in the Weston Park Museum in Sheffield, and they include flint arrow heads, knives and scrapers, scraps of melted bronze and beads, including one of red 'faience' porcelain, which may have come from Egypt.

Nearly all of Stanton Moor's honoured dead were cremated

and interred in pots, as was the custom during the Bronze Age between 1,800 and 1,400 BC.

d Take care as you pass on the perimeter track above the deep gritstone quarries which scar the eastern side of Stanton Moor. There are fine views down into the Derwent Valley to Stanton Lees and Darley Dale through the trees. Several interesting gritstone tors are passed, including the Cat Stone, which has convenient footholds worn into it for climbers. All paths lead to the Earl Grey Tower on the edge of the moor.

C Earl Grey Tower 252636

This isolated landmark is very prominent to travellers entering the Peak District from the south on the A6. It commemorates Earl Charles Grey, the Whig Prime Minister who introduced the Parliamentary Reform Bill in 1832, getting rid of the notorious 'rotten boroughs'. The monument was erected by the Thornhill family of Stanton Hall, who still own Stanton Moor. With no apparent entrance (it was blocked long ago), the tower was always known by my children as 'Rapunzel's Tower'.

e Turn left at the tower over the stile and then right and follow the path through the bracken and birch trees to visit the Nine Ladies Stone Circle and King Stone.

Sheep around Birchover

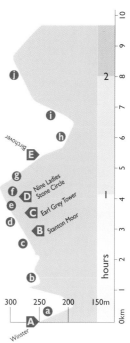

Please note: time taken calculated according to the Naismith formula (see p.2)

D   Nine Ladies Stone Circle 248636

The Nine Ladies Stone Circle, in a clearing in the sparse birchwoods of the moor, is an insignificant ring of low stones dating from the Bronze Age. It was formerly enclosed by a drystone wall, since removed. It is still a focus for 'New Age' visitors, especially around the solstices. The King Stone is an outlying standing stone a few yards to the west, which was recently damaged.

f   Turn left at the Nine Ladies and walk on a broad track across the open heather moorland, passing many heather-covered tumuli and ring cairns en route. Turn right at a junction of paths where you eventually emerge by an old quarry on the right, marked by the curious Cork Stone. This is an apparently natural tor, resting on a much-eroded base and equipped with footholds and handrings for the intrepid climber.

g   Past the Cork Stone, you descend to reach the Stanton-Birchover road. Turn left here and descend past the still-active Birchover Quarry on the left and descend steeply into Birchover via a path which leads off to the right opposite the quarry.

Birchover 238622

Birchover – the appropriate name means 'birch-covered bank' – is a typical one-street village which has grown up in the shadow of Stanton Moor. The Druid Inn, where the path emerges, has a good reputation for its award-winning bar food, and takes its name from the weird outcrops of rock immediately behind the pub. These are known as Rowtor Rocks, and the vivid imagination of the early antiquarians associated their strange formations with the work of druids. Chief among these was the local parson, the Rev. Thomas Eyre, who died in 1717. It was he who carved the amazing collection of caves, rooms, seats and steps which now adorn the rocks, and which offer a fascinating playground, especially for children. He also built the tiny chapel below the rocks, where there are some extraordinary wood carvings, wall paintings, and modern stained glass by the internationally famous artist Brian Clarke, who once lived at the nearby Rectory.

More recently, prehistoric 'cup and ring' carvings have been identified on Rowtor Rocks, which is thought to get its name from a rocking stone at the eastern end of the rocky ridge.

h   Take the lane which runs down past Rowtor Rocks and the church. At a gate take the path which ascends to Rocking

Stone Farm. Follow the path around the farm. The view ahead is eventually dominated by the gritstone outcrops of Cratcliffe Tor and Robin Hood's Stride. This is a fascinating little enclave.

i   Descend to a track, turn left along the track and then down to a stile and across a stream to the B5056 Winster road, which is crossed and the path taken up to Dudwood Lane by a cottage. Turn left on what is one of the oldest roads in the Peak District, known as the 'Portway' – which may date as far back as the Iron Age. It was known as the 'Old Portway' in Saxon times.

j   This rises to cross the B5057 and continues as Islington Lane, which is still on the line of the Portway and past the craggy outcrop of Grey Tor to the A5012 Pikehall road. Turn left at this cross-roads and noting the Miner's Standard pub (see above) to your left, bear right down the lane to walk back down into Winster.

Silver birch wood on Stanton Moor

FROGGATT EDGE

START/FINISH:
Curbar Gap car park, above Curbar village. Trains from Sheffield, Manchester and (less frequent) Stockport at Grindleford, Upper Padley

DISTANCE:
About 11km/7 miles

APPROXIMATE TIME:
Allow 4 hours

HIGHEST POINT:
Curbar Edge 339m/1,112ft

MAPS:
OS Outdoor Leisure Sheet 24, The White Peak: Harveys Dark Peak South

REFRESHMENTS:
At Curbar Gap (in season); pubs at Curbar or Grindleford

ADVICE:
An easy moorland promenade, followed by field and woodland paths

WILDLIFE INTEREST:
Woodpeckers, redstart, pied flycatcher, finches. Fox, badger and common mammals

The walk along Froggatt and Curbar Edges is one of the most popular 'edge' walks in the Peak District. This easy 11km/7 mile walk takes in the best of that with a return through the lovely woodlands which flank the River Derwent back to a mill which was the unlikely double for Colditz Castle in the still-remembered TV series of the same name.

A Curbar Gap 263747

Curbar Gap is the prominent 'notch' in the skyline above the village of Calver (pronounced 'Carver') and separates Curbar from Baslow Edge. Just below the edge, to the right of Bar Lane, the minor road which leads up from Calver are a series of flat gravestones which mark the burials of five members of the Cundy family, who were all victims of the Great Plague from the village in 1632 – 33 years before the more famous outbreak in the village of Eyam, across the Derwent.

a Go through the car park to the gate which gives access to the moorland and edge, which is part of the National Park Authority's Eastern Moors Estate. There are many paths along the edge, but the best views are always from those closest to the edge. These extend southwards towards Baslow Edge and the wooded Chatsworth estate, west across the Derwent to Longstone Moor and the quarries in Stoney Middleton Dale, to Eyam and Eyam Moor, with the prominent TV mast on Sir William Hill. Nearer at hand, note the detached column known as Froggatt Pinnacle, and the various climbing routes which ascend these short but steep faces.

b After 3.2km/2 miles of easy edge-strolling where the track and edge bends north, you pass a small stone circle half-hidden in the heather.

B Stoke Flats Bronze Age landscape 250765

Archaeological research on much of the flatter land like Stoke Flat, to the right, which rises above the Eastern Edges like Froggatt, Baslow, Gardom's and Birchen's Edges, has shown that a sizeable population lived and farmed here during the Bronze Age and possibly before. There is evidence of their clearance cairns, field systems, burial mounds, standing stones and hut circles, in addition to ritual monuments such as the stone circle above Froggatt Edge. A continuing programme of excavation on Gardom's Edge, to the south, has also revealed a large Neolithic enclosure, previously thought to be of Iron Age date. Although many of the fields were obviously for arable use, opinion is divided as to whether these Bronze Age settlements were temporary or seasonal. Certainly, it is thought the climate then was slightly warmer than today's.

c   Descend to a gate and cross a stream near Brookside Buttress and keep to the path heading north and cross the B6054 to descend to cross another small stream. Climb to a stile near the National Trust car park close to the Grouse Inn. Bear left over another stile and descend through Hay Wood on a path which gives access to a lane which leads down to the B6521 near Grindleford Bridge.

C   Grindleford 244775

Grindleford is a nucleated village standing mainly on the right bank of the Derwent, of which it has been an important crossing since medieval times. In the upper part of the village on the Hathersage road at the foot of Sir William Hill, the war memorial is a copy of Eyam's Saxon preaching cross. The 'Sir William' after which the hill is named was Sir William Cavendish, Bess of Hardwick's grandson who fought for the king at Marston Moor in 1644 and lived nearby at Stoke Hall. Just up the B6521 are the twin villages of Nether and Upper Padley, and in the woods of Upper Padley is Padley Chapel, all that remains of Padley Manor, where, in 1588, two Roman Catholic priests who were in hiding were discovered, arrested and taken to Derby where they were hanged, drawn and quartered. There is an annual pilgrimage in celebration of the Padley Martyrs in July.

Climbing evening in Curbar Edge

Curbar Edge looking south-east towards Baslow Edge

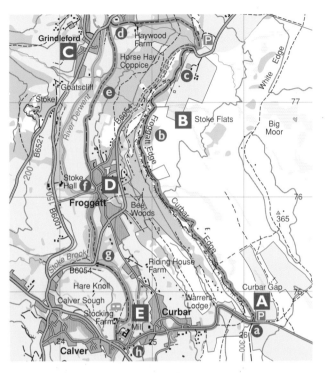

central path, not path to extreme right

d Go left through the gate by the traffic lights over the bridge and follow the path to the right into the woodlands of Horse Hay Coppice and Froggatt Woods. These are delightful, mixed woodlands, full of bird song in the summer, and the lovely path winds in and out between boulders and across gurgling streams running off the moorlands beyond.

e Emerging from the woodland, follow the path across a meadow and into a walled lane which leads past Derwent Farm and into the village of Froggatt.

Grindleford and the Hope Valley from Froggatt Edge

Froggatt Pinnacle and view towards Calver

Please note: time taken calculated according to the Naismith formula (see p.2)

D   Froggatt 243762

The name of Froggatt comes from the Old English and really does mean what it sounds like – 'frog cott or cottage' – a reference to the low-lying ground by the River Derwent in the parish.

Walk 100? m + cross stile to path

f From Froggatt Bridge, take the path which leads beside the banks of the Derwent and follow it to the New Bridge, with its large millpond and weir fed by The Goit across on the opposite bank.

g Eventually the path joins the Duke's Drive – a reference to the Duke of Rutland's route from Haddon to his shooting lodge at Longshaw – which runs into Calver, past the towering presence of Calver Mill.

E   Calver Mill 247745

This imposing late 18th century cotton mill was used to produce stainless steel sinks and equipment. But it gained fame in the 1960s when it served as the model for Colditz Castle in the long-running TV series about the famous German castle used to incarcerate British prisoners of war with a record of escaping from lesser Stalags.

h Turn left from the mill up Curbar Lane and more steeply as it becomes Bar Lane, winding up the hill back towards Curbar Gap and your starting point.

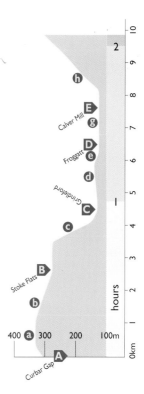

HIGGER TOR AND CARL WARK

START/FINISH:
Longshaw Car Park, (GR 266800) on the B6055 near the Fox House Inn. Served by buses from Sheffield and Castleton

DISTANCE:
About 8km/5 miles

APPROXIMATE TIME:
Allow 3 hours

HIGHEST POINT:
Higger Tor 434m/1,424ft

MAPS:
OS Outdoor Leisure Sheet 1, The Dark Peak; Harveys Dark Peak South

REFRESHMENTS:
At Longshaw Lodge and there is usually a mobile at Upper Burbage Bridge in summer

ADVICE:
Easy moorland paths. Take care on wet and windy days on edges and moorland

WILDLIFE INTEREST:
Red grouse, curlew, meadow pipit. Pied flycatcher, woodpeckers and redstarts in Padley Gorge

The twin tors of Higger and Carl Wark dominate the Upper Burbage Valley which rises above the National Trust's Longshaw Estate and the Fox House Inn. This is a popular arena for school parties and visitors from nearby Sheffield, and is rich in history and legend. The mysterious fortification of Carl Wark has never been satisfactorily explained, but is certainly prehistoric.

A Longshaw Lodge 266800

Haddon's Duke of Rutland built Longshaw Lodge around 1830 as a shooting lodge for visiting house parties intent on bagging as many grouse as they could from the surrounding moors after the 'Glorious Twelfth' of August each year. It is now best known as the venue for one of the Peak's major sheepdog trials, held in September. The National Trust acquired part of the estate when it was sold off in the 1930s, and the house was converted into flats.

The estate is now run as a country park, with visitor centre, shop, restaurant and toilets. The most important area for nature conservation is the old oak and birch woodland of Padley Gorge, downstream from the lodge, which is famous for its population of migrant pied flycatchers in summer.

a   From Longshaw Lodge turn right and go out through the gatehouse. Cross the road (B6521) and take the broad path through the mixed trees and which then runs parallel with the A625 to cross it opposite a small area used for parking. A sign just past here on the road leads to the upper path running along the top of Burbage Rocks on the edge of Burbage Moor.

Footpath northwards along Burbage Valley showing Carl Wark and Higger Tor

b There is a little hiatus in the ridge, where the rocks give way to heather as the path drops down and a path leads right towards Houndkirk Moor. Bear left here to reach the crest of the northern part of Burbage Rocks.

Winter landscape on Higger Tor (towards Burbage Valley)

B Burbage Rocks 268823

Abandoned millstones and grindstones litter the old quarries constructed in the face of Burbage Rocks from where they were fashioned. The industry was very important locally from medieval times, but by 1800 the industry was running down partly because of foreign imports and partly because the Peak millstones made grey flour when white bread was more popular. Many were left where they had been made, such as the large collection at Laurencefield below Millstone Edge.

The former quarries such as Millstone and those at Burbage now make excellent venues for rock climbers, and they are often to be seen struggling below Burbage Rocks.

The views from here extend across the dark plantations in the bottom of the valley of Burbage Brook to the outcrops of Carl Wark and Higger Tor and beyond to the Mam Tor ridge and Win Hill. The broad track which runs below the rocks is known as the Duke's Drive, another reminder of the Duke of Rutland's shooting parties, and is an alternative route.

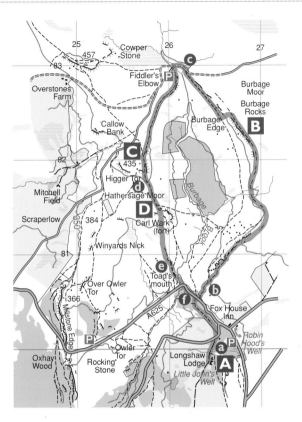

c The edge path is followed all the way to Upper Burbage Bridge, which is seen ahead. Cross the two streams here and contour below the Fiddler's Elbow Road left towards the first rocky slopes of Higger Tor ahead.

C Higger Tor 257820

The rock-fringed plateau of Higger Tor 434m/1,424ft. is punctuated by weird tors of grey gritstone, the most prominent of which is the awesome Leaning Buttress on its southern edge. These are also popular places for climbers who enjoy their vertiginous challenges.

The name simply means 'higher' tor, and must have been originally named by the occupants of Carl Wark, which is now visible on the moor beneath.

d Clamber down through the boulders of Higger on a sandy path which leads across the moor to the impressive entrance to Carl Wark below.

Winter sunset on Higger Tor

Blustery day down the Hope Valley from Higger Tor

D   Carl Wark 259815

The huge stones of the 3m/10ft high monumental wall on three sides of this natural little plateau are very impressive. Usually attributed to the Iron Age and sometimes to as late as the Dark Ages, this formidable defensive position may be as early as the Neolithic, or New Stone Age, according to the latest archaeological theories. Certainly, the moorland between here and Over Owler Tor to the south has revealed extensive prehistoric field systems and clearance cairns, which could well date from as early as that period.

Whatever the date, Carl Wark is one of the finest defensive sites in the Dark Peak, and is a place to stop and admire the 'Carle's Work' as it was named by Camden in 1789.

e   Walk down from Carl Wark on the path which leads from its western end down to the road junction at Toad's Mouth – another weirdly-shaped rock which juts out over the road and bears more than a passing resemblance to its namesake, especially as someone has carved an eye above the mouth!

f   Follow the road left to rejoin the path back to Longshaw Lodge across the road through the trees on the right.

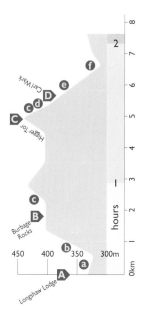

STANAGE EDGE

START/FINISH:
Car park in the centre of Hathersage, which is also served by buses from Sheffield and Bakewell and trains from Sheffield and Stockport

DISTANCE:
About 14km/9 miles

APPROXIMATE TIME:
About 5 hours

HIGHEST POINT:
High Neb, Stanage
458m/1,502ft

MAPS:
OS Outdoor Leisure Sheet 1, The Dark Peak; Harveys Dark Peak South

REFRESHMENTS:
Cafes and pubs in Hathersage

ADVICE:
Mainly on field paths and lanes, with a moorland promenade. Take care on wet, windy or foggy days

WILDLIFE INTEREST:
Lapwing, curlew, red grouse, meadow pipit. Weasel, fox, mountain hare

S tanage Edge is a Mecca for rock climbers from all over Britain. This 6km/4-mile long gritstone escarpment is the classic Peakland 'edge' and has over 850 climbing routes up its short but steep faces. This walk ascends the edge from Hathersage, alleged last resting place of Little John, passes North Lees Hall of Brontë fame, and visits Robin Hood's Cave on Stanage, so has much of literary interest.

A Hathersage 230815

Hathersage is a busy, prosperous village on the A625 between Sheffield and the Hope Valley. In the 19th century, it was the home of a thriving needle, pin and wire-drawing industry, now disappeared, although the old mill buildings still remain. Many men were also employed on mill and grindstone making, and the remains of their industry, in the form of abandoned stones, is still very evident beneath the rock faces of Stanage and other edges.

But perhaps Hathersage's main, if dubious, claim to fame is the abnormally long 'grave' just outside the church porch, which is claimed to be that of Robin Hood's faithful lieutenant Little John, who is said to have come from Hathersage in some versions of this long-lived legend. The church itself, mainly 14th and 15th centuries, has many more demonstrable monuments to members of the Eyre family, the local lords of

Hathersage and Stanage Edge behind

the manor, inside, and a chancel window which was rescued from the now-submerged Derwent church.

Stanage Edge looking north at Crow Chin

Beyond the church, the mysterious earthworks of Camp Green tell of an even earlier occupation and probably date from the Dark Ages.

a From the centre of the village, walk due north up Baulk Lane, which soon reverts to a clear track after passing over a cattle grid. Crossing a couple of stiles, the path keeps above the Hood Brook and passes through the grounds of Brookfield Manor and enters a narrow walled path. This eventually leads to a minor road, where you turn right, and then left up the drive to North Lees Hall.

B North Lees Hall 235834

This fine Tudor tower house dates from the last years of the 16th century and was one of the homes of the Eyre family, who are said to have come to England with the Conqueror. It is said that Robert Eyre, the patriarch of the family who lived across the valley at the quaintly-named Highlow Hall, built a hall for each of his seven sons within sight of his own house, and North Lees was one of these.

North Lees Hall, which now provides exclusive holiday accommodation, is also thought to have been the model which Charlotte Brontë used for Thornfield Hall in her novel Jane Eyre. It is known that Charlotte often visited her good friend, Ellen Nussey, who lived at the Hathersage Vicarage, and knew the area and its families well. The North Lees estate, including its camp site, is owned by the National Park Authority, and the estate is farmed by the Derbyshire College of Agriculture.

b Pass through the farmyard of North Lees and follow the path upwards towards Stanage Edge, which is now ahead. Go up through the trees by a stream to emerge at the road beneath Stanage Edge, turning left and then right before reaching the Hollin Bank car park, to ascend a path leading up towards the edge.

c This paved route is known as Jacob's Ladder and leads through the scattered pines of the Stanage Plantation to climb through a weakness in the crags to reach the top of the edge.

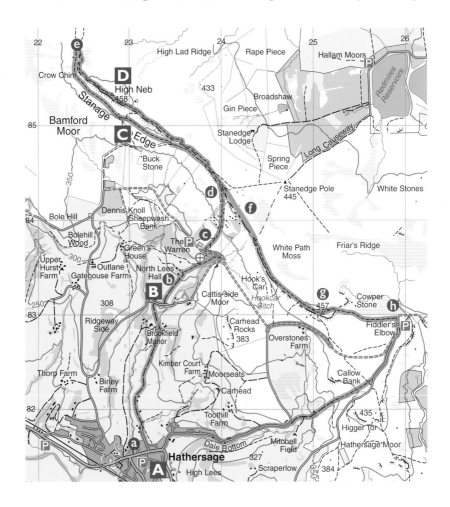

North Lees Hall

Please note: time taken calculated according to the Naismith formula (see p.2)

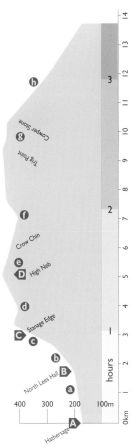

C   Stanage Edge 237844

On a sunny Sunday afternoon, Stanage Edge can resemble Piccadilly Circus, with the 6km/4-mile escarpment of grey gritstone festooned with colourful climbers' ropes and even more colourful climbers, while overhead, hang-gliders soar in the thermals. There are climbing routes of all standards here, from the test pieces set up in the Fifties by climbers like Joe Brown and Don Whillans, to the easier routes for beginners, many of whom come from the surrounding cities and will have started their climbing here. The first climbs on Stanage were done in before the First World War, but it was working class climbers like Brown and Whillans who really opened it up, with classic routes like the Right Unconquerable and Manchester Buttress.

d Follow the edge-top path left which descends as the Long Causeway joins it from the right from the landmark of Stanage Pole. Keep to the edge which gradually climbs through the rocks and heather to the high point of High Neb, and its trig point.

D   High Neb 228853

'Neb' is a Northern word meaning 'nose' and this 458m/1,502ft blunt nose of gritstone forms the high point of the Stanage Edge escarpment. The view from here is justly popular among walkers, although the further north you go on Stanage, the fewer climbers you will encounter. A few steps further takes you to Crow Chin, where the Stanage escarpment turns north by the remains of two ancient burial cairns.

The view westwards is over the Derwent Valley and up to Win Hill and Lose Hill, with the broad Bamford Moor forming the foreground and the long line of the Kinder Scout plateau, with Bleaklow beyond, the horizon.

Millstones below Stanage

e You have a choice of routes to return to Jacob's Ladder, either retracing your steps along the edge top path, or dropping down from Crow Chin along the path which winds between the boulders and discarded millstones back to the paved track.

View towards Win and Lose Hill with millstones in foreground

f Whichever way you take, return to the edge top path at Jacob's Ladder and continue along the edge of White Path Moss, with extensive views across the Derwent Valley to Hathersage and Offerton Moor beyond. You soon pass the gritstone balcony cut into the edge known as Robin Hood's Cave on your right.

g Passing the trig. point (457m/1,499 ft) at the end of the main escarpment, head for the Cowper Stone but cross the moor to head for the Ringlowling road, reaching it near Upper Burbage Bridge. The valley of the Burbage Brook is ahead.

h Turn right and descend on the Fiddler's Elbow road over a cattle grid and, with Higger Tor ahead, take the right hand path which leads across Callow Bank to a stile into a walled lane on the left. This ascends to the road junction at Mitchell Fold where you descend on this lane for an easy 1.6km/1 mile down Dale Bottom and back into Hathersage again.

THE ROACHES AND LUD'S CHURCH

START/FINISH:
Limited roadside parking areas near Rockhall Cottage, served on summer weekends by a park and ride service from Tittesworth Reservoir

DISTANCE:
About 11km/7 miles

APPROXIMATE TIME:
Allow at least 4 hours

HIGHEST POINT:
Roach End, 505m/1,657ft

MAPS:
OS Outdoor Leisure Sheet 24, The White Peak

REFRESHMENTS:
At Tittesworth Reservoir, café at Paddock Farm, pubs at Meerbrook, Upper Hulme and Blockshow Moor, and occasionally a roadside van beneath the Roaches

ADVICE:
Quite a strenuous ridge and moorland ramble, finishing on forest paths

WILDLIFE INTEREST:
Red grouse, golden plover, curlew, ring ouzel. Redstart, finches in woodland, dipper. Badger, fox, brown hare, mosses in Lud's Church

The Roaches, Hen Cloud and Ramshaw Rocks syncline is a classic landscape formation which dominates the western arm of the Dark Peak. Popular with climbers, these sharp little cliffs of pink-hued grit enclose a secret self-contained landscape where, in the depths of Back Forest, the mysterious chasm of Lud's Church has attracted its own myths and legends.

A The Roaches 004621

The name 'Roaches' simply means rocks, and comes from the Norman French 'roches'. This spectacular landscape has attracted attention ever since Dr. Robert Plot wrote in his *Compleat History of Staffordshire* (1730): Here are also vast Rocks which surprise with Admiration, called the Henclouds and Leek Roches. They are of so great a height and afford such stupendous Prospects that one could hardly believe they were anywhere to be found but in Picture.

Formed of layers of pinkish millstone grit and softer shales, the area is a classic syncline, or downfold in the landscape, with the lower-lying coal measures of Goldsitch Moss lying in the centre. This is best seen from the sharp little summit of Hen Cloud (410m/1,345ft) which lies at the apex of the downfold.

The various tiers of The Roaches provide some of the finest and longest gritstone climbs in the Peak District, including test piece routes such as the fearsome overhanging roof of The Sloth, first climbed by Don Whillans in 1954 and so named because of the amount of time spent hanging upside down, and the equally-descriptive The Mincer (Joe Brown, 1950).

Tucked away under the overhanging rocks of the Roaches is the former gamekeeper's cottage partly built into the cliff face and known as Rock Hall. It is now a climbers' bothy but was formerly occupied by the eccentric Dougie Moller, the self-styled 'Lord of the Roaches'.

a From the parking areas follow the road towards Upper Hulme until you reach a broad track on the left which leads up towards the col between The Roaches and Hen Cloud, which stands like a miniature Rock of Gibraltar to your right.

(If you have time, the ascent of Hen Cloud is a worthy addition to the walk, if only for the marvellous view of the Roaches syncline).

b Turn left at the col and follow the boundary wall taking the higher path which leads towards the lower tier of crags, surmounted through gaps in the rocks to reach the upper tier. (The lower path ends up below the cliff faces of Rock Hall, and the ridge can be gained by a steep climb through the rocks.) There is a fine view from here back towards Hen Cloud and over the Staffordshire Plain towards the glinting waters of Tittesworth Reservoir.

c The route now follows the crest of the Roaches ridge on a superb promenade with extensive views to the left through the impressive rock buttress before ascending to the peaty hollow which contains Doxey Pool.

Rock formations on the Roaches

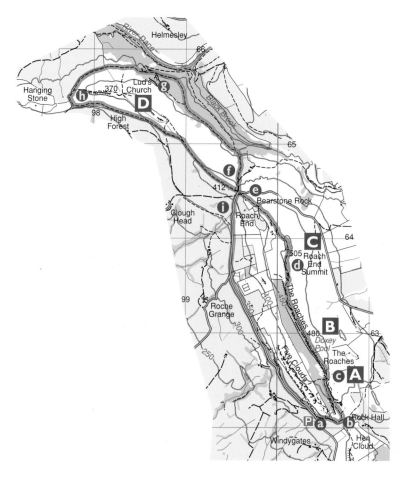

B   Doxey Pool 004628

Like so many physical features in the Staffordshire moorlands, Doxey Pool has its legends. This shallow, peaty pool is said to have no inlet nor outlet, and is the home of a seductive siren of a mermaid, who attracts unwise young men to a watery grave. After she had been abducted from the pool, she returned to haunt the scene. Other stories tell of a fearsome green monster that lurks in the murky depths. The name of Doxey Pool is recorded in the Domesday Book as 'Dochesig'; the last part of the name means a watercourse, while 'Doche' may refer to a long-lost personal name.

d From Doxey Pool, the path starts a gradual ascent towards the trig. point at the summit of The Roaches ridge (505m/1,675ft).

Rock Hall or The Whillans Hut below the Roaches

Please note: time taken calculated according to the Naismith formula (see p.2)

C   Roach End summit 001639

The views from here are extensive, especially looking north west, where the shapely cone of Shutlingsloe rises above the valley of the River Dane. Due west, The Cloud above Congleton is prominent ('clud' is an Old English word which, like the Roaches, means a rock or hill)'.

There are some wonderful examples of wind and frost erosion among the weird tors and outcrops of rock below here, including one marked on the OS map as Bearstone Rock. Which one it is anyone's guess. Other rocks show distinctive sedimentary banding where the grits were laid down at different angles.

e   A series of worn steps lead down to the minor road at Roach End. Turn right here and then left through a stile which leads down through the heather and rocks towards the trees of Back Forest and Forest Wood in the valley below.

f   After crossing a ditch walk up the bank towards a signpost. Turn left here and keep to the ridge top leading through the lovely mixed woodland, with occasional aerial

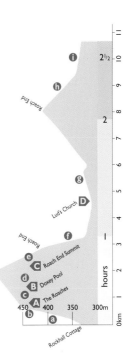

Grouse on moorland

views down to the rushing waters of the Black Brook beneath you through the pines to the right. After about 800m/½ mile, you reach a sign in a clearing which points the way to the partly concealed sunken entrance to Lud's Church.

D   Lud's Church 987656
Although described on the map as a cave, Lud's Church is really a large landslip, lost among the trees of Forest Wood. It is a spectacular rift, and one of the most atmospheric and evocative places in the Peak. The chasm is 18m /60ft deep and dog-legs into the hillside, dripping with ferns and mosses and usually very damp and muddy underfoot.

It is small wonder that this awesome ravine should attract legends, the oldest of which associates it with the Green Chapel in the medieval Arthurian alliterative poem *Sir Gawain and the Green Knight*. It has been suggested that this was where Gawain meets up with the knight to perform a beheading ritual, which has Celtic echoes and may even predate the late 14th century poem. The name of the chasm is said to come from Walter de Lud Auk, a 14th century supporter of Wycliffe who held services in this secret place, far away from the eyes of authority.

g   Having passed through Lud's Church, you emerge at the other end and take the sandy path which leads through ancient oak woodland to the gritstone outcrop known as Castle Cliff Rocks, which overlooks the Upper Dane Valley. The hillside opposite is Tagsclough Hill.

h   Walking west again, take the concessionary path signposted Roach End which leads off left across scrub and moorland, with good views towards Shutlingsloe. This path climbs along the top of the moor to a marshy col, and then on alongside a wall.

i   Back at Roach End, turn right and follow the gated minor road which leads pleasantly beneath the rocky escarpments of the Roaches and the closer Five Clouds for just over 1.6km/1 mile back to your starting point near Rock Hall. The attractive views to the right across the green pastures towards Gun Hill and Tittesworth are constant companions.

Rock Hall

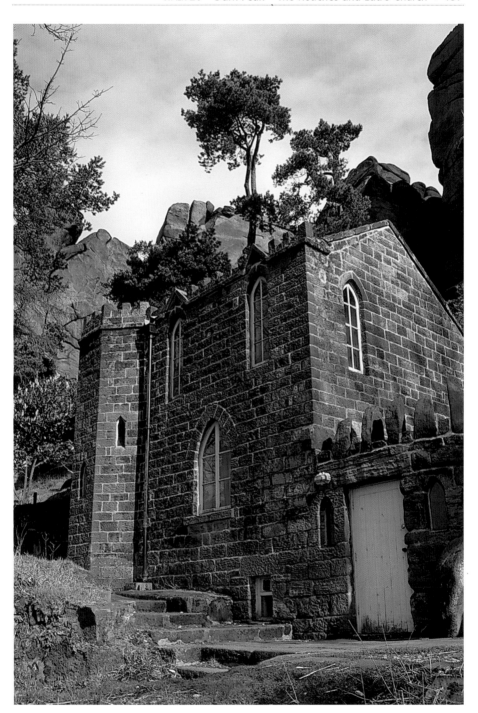

SHUTLINGSLOE

START/FINISH:
North West Water's Trentabank car park, on the minor road to Macclesfield Forest east of Langley

DISTANCE:
10km/6 miles

APPROXIMATE TIME:
Allow 3–4 hours

HIGHEST POINT:
Shutlingsloe, 506m/1,660ft

MAP:
OS Outdoor Leisure Sheet 24, The White Peak

REFRESHMENTS:
Occasionally at Trentabank, pub in Wildboarclough. Hanging Gate Inn on route near the end of the walk

ADVICE:
A steep, but paved, hill climb, then field and moorland paths which can be wet. Take care on descents when wet

WILDLIFE INTEREST:
Heronry at Trentabank Reservoir, wildfowl including great crested grebe, red-breasted merganser and goldeneye on reservoir. Goldcrest, woodpeckers and finches in forest. Birds of prey, including buzzard and kestrel. Fallow deer in forest

Shutlingsloe summit looking south-east

An over-enthusiastic guidebook author once dubbed Shutlingsloe 'the Matterhorn of the Peak'. Although this may be something of an exaggeration, this shapely hill which pokes its craggy, crooked summit above the conifers of Macclesfield Forest is one of the few real peaks worthy of the name in the Peak District. This pleasant walk also takes in the charming village of Wildboarclough.

A Trentabank Reservoir 961711

The log cabin-style visitor centre and ranger briefing centre at Trentabank Reservoir in the heart of the conifers of Macclesfield Forest gives more than a hint of 'Rose Marie' to the start of this walk. Trentabank Reservoir was constructed in 1929 to supply clear Pennine water to Macclesfield and district, and is now managed by North West Water. The water company and the National Park have constructed an excellent nature trail suitable for disabled people down to the reservoir. Unlike many reservoirs, Trentabank has a variety of wildlife interest, most important of which is the large heronry, visible from the roadside, which is managed by the Cheshire Wildlife Trust. Goldeneye, red-breasted mergansers and great crested grebe also frequent the secluded waters of the reservoir.

a Turn right from the visitor centre on a path which runs alongside the road before turning right into a track (following signs to Shutlingsloe) which ascends steeply in places through the conifers of Macclesfield Forest. At the edge of the

forest turn right to follow the Wall to High Moor. This is a concessionary path.

Path leading to Shutlingsloe summit from Macclesfield Forest

b   Once out of the forest, the track becomes paved as it crosses High Moor, with our objective of Shutlingsloe looking increasingly inviting ahead. The paving was laid by Cheshire County Council and the National Park in 1992 to overcome severe erosion problems on the path as it crosses the soft ground of High Moor. A helicopter was used to transport the re-used slabs which had been taken from derelict Lancashire cotton mills.

c   The path turns right to follow a wall to a ladder stile just beneath the last, steep climb up the northern face of Shutlingsloe, through a staircase of outcropping sandstone crags to the ridgetop summit.

B   Shutlingsloe 976695

The 506m/1,660ft summit of Shutlingsloe is one of the finest in the Peak, with spectacular views eastwards across the wooded valley of Wildboarclough to Axe Edge and Oliver Hill, and north towards Shining Tor and distant Kinder Scout. To the south, the rocky escarpments of the Roaches and Ramshaw Rocks are prominent, while the broad Cheshire

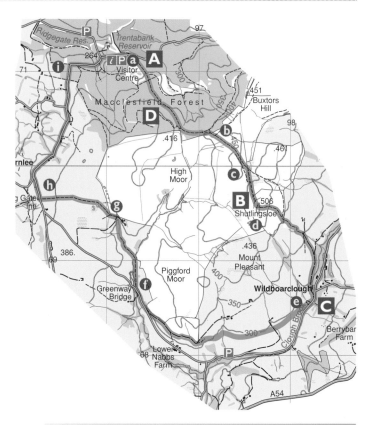

Mist rising below Shutlingsloe

Shutlingsloe from Wildboarclough

Plain, with Macclesfield in the foreground, fills the western view. On a clear day, the dish of the Jodrell Bank Radio Telescope can be seen.

The unusual name of Shutlingsloe is thought to mean 'Scyttel's Hill', and its craggy summit provides the exciting denouement to local man Alan Garner's classic children's fantasy, The Weirdstone of Brisingamen. There is a memorial toposcope on the craggy summit.

d   A waymark on the summit points the way down towards the next objective, the village of Wildboarclough. After a steep little scramble requiring special care, the path emerges at a stile above Shutlingsloe Farm, which is bypassed. The farm drive is then joined and followed down to the lane which leads right to drop down to the road. The route continues right but Wildboarclough itself is on the left and over the bridge.

C   Wildboarclough 984687
The old name of the scattered hamlet of Wildboarclough was Crag, and this name is recalled in the name of the Crag Inn, a popular hostelry passed on the route.

Wildboarclough's other claim to fame, other than the mineral water now produced in its name, is its former Post Office, which must have been one of the largest and most grandiose in the country. Crag Mill, now used for residential accommodation, is a splendid 18th century Georgian-style

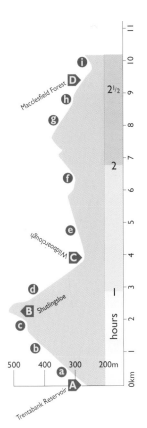

Please note: time taken calculated according to the Naismith formula (see p.2)

building which started life as the manager's house and administration block for Crag Mill, which spun silk for the Great Exhibition of 1851. The little church of St. Saviour dates from the early years of the century.

e From the Cragg Inn car park, take a stile on your right and follow the lovely path which contours around the gorse-dotted slopes of aptly-named Mount Pleasant. After passing Higher Nabbs Farm bear right across a field to reach a walled track and continue along here until you reach the road again just before Greenway Bridge. The obvious path going to Lower Nabbs Farm is not a public path.

f Before reaching the bridge, turn right at a stile and follow the bank of Oaken Clough to cross a slab bridge. Continue at the side of the Clough. At a ruined hut a concessionary path runs alongside a pond to join the house drive. Turn right and then immediately left up a fenced path to a stile which leads across High Moor.

g Follow this path to the corner of the moor and a stile which leads down on a walled path to emerge onto the road at the Hanging Gate public house. This pub used to have a somewhat unwelcoming sign which read:

> This gate hangs here
> and troubles none
> refresh and pay
> and travel on

h Turn right and keep right at a sharp hairpin in the main road. On this minor road pass Brownlow Farm, Higher Hardings Farm and the delightfully-named Thickwithens (all on the right). There are extensive views ahead over the conifers of Macclesfield Forest towards the prominent neb of Tegg's Nose.

D   Macclesfield Forest 965710

The original Forest of Macclesfield was a hunting ground for the Earls of Chester during the Middle Ages, and today's regimented conifers are still the home of fox, badger, tawny owls, woodpeckers and Britain's tiniest bird, the goldcrest.

i As the road descends back into the trees, keep right at a sharp bend and drop down steeply. At a T-junction turn right back towards Trentabank, and the start at the car park.

Towards Oakenclough from below Shutlingsloe

THE GOYT VALLEY

START/FINISH:
Errwood Hall car park
(012748), Goyt Valley, where
the road between The Street
and Derbyshire Bridge is closed
at summer weekends to
through traffic

DISTANCE:
10km/6 miles

APPROXIMATE TIME:
Allow 3–4 hours

HIGHEST POINT:
Shining Tor 559m/1,834ft

MAPS:
OS Outdoor Leisure Sheet 24,
The White Peak

REFRESHMENTS:
Sometimes there is a mobile
unit in Errwood car park in
summer

ADVICE:
Forestry and moorland
walking, nothing too strenuous

WILDLIFE INTEREST:
Hen harrier, migrant osprey,
merlin, grouse on moors.
Wildfowl, great crested grebe,
mergansers on reservoir.
Woodpecker, nuthatch in
woodlands, plus fox, badger

The Goyt Valley is the Dark Peak in microcosm. It has the lot: fine heather moorlands, plantation woodlands, reservoirs and a history of human occupation which has changed radically over the years. This walk takes in the best of the Goyt Valley, a popular resort for the citizens of Stockport and the towns west of the Peak District, and the scene of a pioneering traffic management scheme in the early 1970s.

A   Errwood and Fernilee Reservoirs 015754 and 013770
The Fernilee Reservoir was built in 1938 to supply water to Stockport. It is the larger of the two and contains 1,087

million gallons. It was followed by the 927 million gallon Errwood Reservoir higher up the valley opposite the car park, in 1968. Errwood is used by a thriving sailing club, whose clubhouse is on the opposite shore of the reservoir from the car park, and it is also used by anglers.

a   Leave the car park by taking the Forestry Commission nature trail path. Almost immediately take a right fork and climb up to meet the trees at a small gap in the wall. Crossing a stream, you soon come to a sign for the romantic ruins of Errwood Hall.

B   Errwood Hall 008748

Errwood Hall was the Italianate country mansion of the Grimshawe family, built in 1830 by Samuel Grimshawe as a wedding present for his son. Here, the Grimshawes lived 'in

Looking across Errwood Reservoir from above Errwood Hall

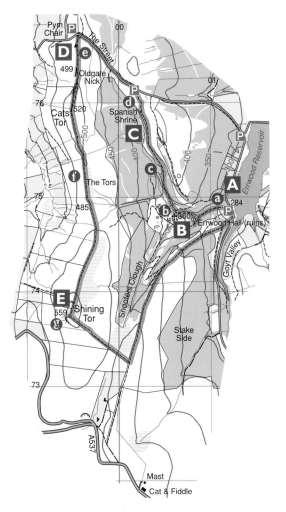

the style of foreign princes' according to a contemporary account, on a huge estate which they planted with 40,000 rhododendron and azalea bushes brought to England by their ocean-going yacht, the *Mariquita*. Modern visitors are still receiving the benefits of the Grimshawe's collecting zeal, for the woods at the back of the car park are ablaze with blooms in the early summer. The hall was partly demolished in the interests of water purity in 1938, when the Fernilee Reservoir was built.

b Walking past the ruins take the path to the left through the forest. Cross a stream and walk up the bank to a signpost at a path intersection. The Grimshawe's burial ground is now behind you and to your left on top of a partially wooded hillock. This is worth a short detour to look at the graves which include Captain John Butler of the *Mariquita*. To continue the walk return to the signpost and take the path for 'The Shrine, Pym Chair' which leads upwards beneath Foxlow Edge.

C   The Spanish Shrine 002759
This isolated building was erected by the Grimshawe family in 1889 as a memorial to their much-loved governess, Dolores de Bergrin, the daughter of a Spanish aristocrat, who had died in her early forties. The shrine is dedicated to San José, and features a beautiful altar backed by a colourful mosaic. There are always fresh flowers in this touching little chapel.

c   Continue up the steep path to meet the road, known as The Street. This is an ancient way which may have been a Roman road from the west into Buxton, and was certainly later used as a salters' way for traders bringing the precious commodity from Cheshire into the Peak District.

d   Turn left to climb steadily up to the summit of the road at Pym Chair, where there is a sign for Shining Tor.

D   Pym Chair 995766
Although nothing remains of the original rock after which this

Errwood Reservoir

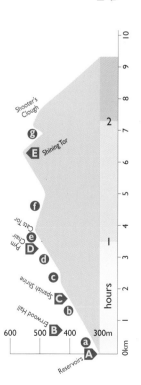

Please note: time taken calculated according to the Naismith formula (see p.2)

Ruins of Errwood Hall, the Goyt
Valley

place is named, this was a landmark on the ancient route still emphatically-known as The Street. It may have been named after John Pym, the 17th century Puritan and Parliamentarian leader. There are fine views westwards from here across the Cheshire Plain towards wooded Alderley Edge, and beyond that to the dim hills of Wales. Eastwards, across the deep defile of the Goyt, Combs Moss fills the horizon.

e Turn left here and follow the reconstructed moorland path beside the wall, which soon dips to Oldgate Nick, where the hollow ways of numerous packhorse trails used to cross the ridge. It leads steadily upward to the summit of 519m/1,703ft Cats Tor – apparently named after the wild cats which formerly haunted this high ridge.

f From here the route dips again down to the col known as The Tors and then steadily up again to the high point of the walk on the broad summit of Shining Tor, reached by crossing the wall by a ladder stile.

E Shining Tor 994737
The 559m/1,834ft summit of Shining Tor is the highest point in Cheshire and in the western arm of the Dark Peak, and the view from its summit is extensive. It takes in the dark conifers

of Macclesfield Forest, watched over by the shapely summit of Shutlingsloe, and also the great white saucer of the Jodrell Bank Radio Telescope can usually be seen on the broad Cheshire Plain over to the west. Nearer at hand, the isolated hostelry of the Cat and Fiddle Inn on the main Buxton-Macclesfield road is watched over by its associated radio mast. Shining Tor is a popular venue for hang gliders, and if the weather and wind conditions are right, several will be seen swooping from the top.

g   Turn back over the wall and continue along the path, descending on a sometimes wet path down past the head of Shooter's Clough and up to a stile. Here you turn left to descend on the ridge above the clough on your left on a fine green track which leads down to the valley road near the starting point at the Errwood car park. There are fine views ahead over the Errwood Reservoir.

Hang-glider coming into land on Shining Tor

THE GREAT RIDGE

START/FINISH:
Mam Nick Car Park, off the
A625 west of Castleton

DISTANCE:
8km/5 miles

APPROXIMATE TIME:
Allow 2½–3½ hours

HIGHEST POINT:
Mam Tor, 517m/1,695ft

MAPS:
OS Outdoor Leisure Sheet 1,
The Dark Peak; Harveys, Dark
Peak North and South

REFRESHMENTS:
Near Blue John Mine (mobile)
or pubs and cafes in Castleton

ADVICE:
Easy paths, paved for much of
the way

WILDLIFE INTEREST:
Skylark, meadow pipit,
lapwing, curlew

It appears to have been the late Walter (W.A.) Poucher who was the first to emphatically call the Mam Tor-Lose Hill ridge 'the Great Ridge', in his *Peak and Pennines* guide, first published in 1966. The name is now widely accepted for this classic, 3.2km/2-mile promenade along the shale and grit ridge which stands on the borders of the Dark and White Peaks, and looks into the hearts of both.

a   Take the steps which lead up from the back of the Mam Nick car park and follow the path rising gradually through the trees to emerge at a stile which leads to more urban-looking stone-paved steps which pass through the ramparts defending the western spur of Mam Tor.

A   Mam Tor 127836

Mam Tor, 517m/1,695ft high and 6ha/16 acres in area, is one of the highest, largest and most easily attained hill forts in the Pennines, and certainly the most impressively situated. The name may be Celtic and mean 'Mother Mountain', and the bald, windswept summit certainly exerts a certain matriarchal dominance over the head of the Hope Valley above Castleton.

Originally thought to date, like most hill forts, from the Iron Age, excavations at Mam Tor have found pottery which indicated a much earlier, late Bronze Age date for the substantial double ramparts and the numerous hut circles

Rushup Edge and Dalehead
from Mam Tor

The Great Ridge from Back Tor towards Mam Tor

which pit the interior. Archaeologists now doubt that such 'forts' had a purely military purpose. They may have been used as meeting places or summer sheilings from where stock could be watched as it grazed the neighbouring hills. The much-eroded tumulus (burial mound) which marked the summit has recently been completely encased by the National Trust in stone cobbles, which many visitors take for the real thing.

The other popular name for Mam Tor is 'the Shivering Mountain', a reference to the unstable layers of shale and grit which have slipped away from the east face, creating a chocolate-cake appearance when viewed from Castleton. These shales are still slipping, and looking down from the summit, the huge mass of landslipped debris which has fallen from the face can be seen spreading down towards Castleton in a huge fan. Hang gliders and parascenders use Mam Tor as

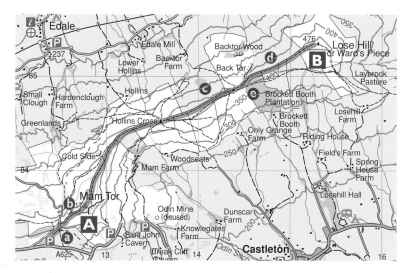

a launch point in the right conditions, adding more colourful interest to the summit.

The views from Mam Tor are justly famous, extending along the sinuous line of the Great Ridge to Back Tor and Lose Hill, east down the length of the Hope Valley, with Castleton and its castle prominent in the foreground, and west towards the moorland heights of Lord's Seat and Brown Knoll. Kinder Scout, and the booths of Edale, fill the northern view, with Grindslow Knoll prominent above Grindsbrook.

b   Take the broad, flag-stoned path which leads north through the ramparts of Mam Tor and down to the memorial topograph at the col of Hollins Cross. This was a stopping place on the 'coffin route' for the deceased of Edale being taken to Castleton for burial. (You can shorten the route by taking the path to Castleton from here, but you will face the long climb up The Winnats or the A625 to return to the car park).

c   Continue along the ridge to the foot of Back Tor and climb up the badly-eroded and loose path to the summit. Back Tor is a kind of Mam Tor in reverse, for in this case the landslipped face points north-west. It is an impressive, but terribly lose, crag, with the scraggy remains of Brockett Booth Plantation climbing its smooth southern slopes.

d   From Back Tor, the path descends slightly again before the final climb, again on paving slabs, to the graceful summit of Lose Hill.

B   Lose Hill 153854

The 476m/1,563ft summit of Lose (pronounced 'Loose') Hill is more properly known as Ward's Piece, in honour of G.H.B. 'Bert' Ward, the so-called 'King of the Clarion Ramblers'. This remarkable Sheffielder was a great campaigner for open access to the then-forbidden moors of the Dark Peak, and almost single-handed wrote and published the wonderfully-meticulous little Sheffield Clarion Ramblers Handbooks for more than 50 years until his death in 1957. On an April day in 1945 in the presence of a crowd of 2,000 ramblers, the summit and 22 ha/54 acres of the eastern side of Lose Hill were presented to Bert Ward. He immediately handed the deeds to the National Trust so that, as he said: 'This piece of land will belong to everybody for all times'.

The view from Lose Hill looks east across the valley of the Noe to its neighbour, Win Hill and north across Edale to Jagger's Clough and Crookstone Knoll at the eastern end of the Kinder plateau. To the south, Castleton and the white exclamation mark of the chimney of the Hope Valley Cement Works are the most prominent landmarks.

e   Retrace your steps from Lose Hill for a return route of entirely different views from those you met on the outward trip. Cross Back Tor and Hollins Cross to Mam Tor and then down to the Mam Nick car park.

Please note: time taken calculated according to the Naismith formula (see p.2)

Landslip at the foot of Mam Tor

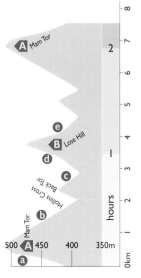

WIN HILL

START/FINISH:
Car park in Hope (1.2km/¾ mile from start), which is served by trains from Stockport and Sheffield on the Hope Valley line and buses from Sheffield

DISTANCE:
9km/5 miles

APPROXIMATE TIME:
Allow 3–4 hours

HIGHEST POINT:
Win Hill 462m/1,518ft

MAPS:
OS Outdoor Leisure Sheet 1, The Dark Peak; Harveys, Dark Peak South

REFRESHMENTS:
Cafes and pubs in Hope

ADVICE:
A stiff climb to a fine summit

WILDLIFE INTEREST:
Grouse, curlew, meadow pipit. Fox, rabbit, hare, kestrel

The 462m/1,518ft summit of Win Hill Pike is one of the finest viewpoints in the Peak District, encompassing the Ladybower Reservoir and Derwent Moors with Bleaklow behind to the north and the wide sweep of the Hope Valley and the first hills of the White Peak to the south. This pleasant half-day walk goes up from the village of Hope, which gave its name to the valley.

A Hope 172835

Although only a tiny village now dominated by the massive cement works at its western end, Hope was once important enough to give its name to one of the key central valleys of the Dark Peak. In 1068, its huge parish took in two-thirds of the Royal Forest of the Peak, including Buxton, Tideswell and Chapel-en-le-Frith. The mainly 13th and 14th century parish church has two 13th century graveslabs which are thought to commemorate officers of the Forest and there is a Saxon cross shaft in the churchyard.

Another echo of Hope's past importance is the weekly livestock market, granted in 1715, and a famous agricultural show and sheepdog trials in August which still attract loyal farmers from the surrounding hills. There is a pinfold in the Pindale Road where stray stock were impounded until their owners could be traced.

a Leave the centre of the village and head down the Edale Road beside the Old Hall pub. After about 400m/¼ mile, turn right and descend on a lane to Killhill Bridge across the River Noe. After passing under a railway bridge, turn right on a track which ascends towards Twitchill Farm.

The Great Ridge and Hope Cross with cyclists

Path leading up to Win Hill

b Above the farm there is a steel gate. Go straight on and up until you reach a stile, keep going straight on until a clear path bears to the right and mounts unrelentingly towards the skyline ridge. Turn right here at the top of Hope Brink, and climb up through the heather on a sandy path towards the beckoning crags of Win Hill Pike.

B Win Hill Pike 188851
Seen from the Hope Valley, Win Hill looks like a shapeless lump, so it is always a pleasant surprise to see that the actual summit really is a rocky little 'pike'. There are many legends concerning how the hill got its name, the most fanciful of which is that the victors in a Dark Age battle encamped here – hence 'Win' Hill – while the losers chose 'Lose' Hill across the Noe opposite. Etymologists, however, are less romantic and believe the name comes from Old English for 'withy' or willow hill.

The view from the 462m/1,518ft summit is wonderful, looking north deep into the Upper Derwent Valley across the blue waters of Ladybower and on towards the tors of Derwent Edge and Bleaklow, and west to the reigning 'Mother Mountain' of Mam Tor at the end of the sinuous Great Ridge which runs from shapely Lose Hill. Kinder Scout and Brown Knoll fill the background. To the south, the view is across the broad, pastoral reaches of the Hope Valley to the Shatton Moor and Bradwell Edge, and the undulating White Peak plateau. The so-called 'Corn Law Rhymer', Ebenezer Elliott , perhaps went a little over the top with his effusive description of Win Hill: 'Star-loved, and meteor-sought, and tempest-found! Proud centre of a mountain-circle, hail!' but it's nevertheless a fine summit.

Heather and gorse on Win Hill

c   After admiring the fine view from the summit, retrace your steps down to the col of Hope and Thornhill Brinks and continue west gently descending the broad ridge following a wall towards Wooler Knoll on the edge of the conifers of Wiseman Hey Clough Plantation.

C   Wooler Knoll 171862

This insignificant 382m/1,253ft summit, almost smothered by the encroaching conifers, marks a narrowing on the ridge which runs down to the ancient guidepost of Hope Cross, where the ghosts of Roman soldiers have allegedly been seen marching up their road from *Navio* (Brough) to   (near Glossop). The name of Wooler Knoll is thought to come from the Old English 'wulf hlaw', meaning 'Wolves' Hill'.

d Just after the summit and the cross-ridge wall, turn sharply left down the bridleway coming up from Hope and descend to join the Roman Road above Harrop Farm. There are grand views from this airy track across the Noe Valley to the dominating slopes of Lose Hill opposite, occasionally enlivened by the sight of trains plying the Hope Valley line in the valley bottom beneath.

D   The Hope Valley Line
The Hope Valley, still a vital artery and a spectacular way to reach the fine walking in the Hope and Edale Valleys, was opened for passengers by the Midland Railway in 1894. It was a difficult line to build and involved the construction of the Cowburn and Totley Tunnels, the latter of which was one of the longest in Britain at 5km/3½ miles. Seven hundred navvies worked on the line, and 30 million bricks were used to line the tunnel, from which 11.4 million l/2.5 million gallons of water had to be extracted from the workings daily. Today, the line is known as 'the Ramblers' Route' and provides a convenient link across the Pennines between Sheffield and Stockport/Manchester.

e Join the walled lane which leads down to Fullwood Stile Farm, which is passed through to a stile which leads south past The Homestead to go under the railway and back to Killhill Bridge again and into Hope along the Edale Road.

Path to the summit of Win Hill

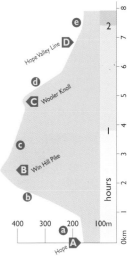

Please note: time taken calculated according to the Naismith formula (see p.2)

KINDER SOUTH AND THE WOOLPACKS

START/FINISH:
Upper Booth, Edale. Edale village (Grindsbrook Booth) is served by trains from Stockport and Sheffield

DISTANCE:
About 8km/5 miles

APPROXIMATE TIME:
Allow 3–4 hours

HIGHEST POINT:
Crowden Tower, 619m/2,030ft

MAPS:
OS Outdoor Leisure Sheet 1, The Dark Peak; Harveys, Dark Peak North

REFRESHMENTS:
Cafe and pubs in Edale village

ADVICE:
A shorter moorland walk, but waterproofs, map and compass needed. It includes a stiff climb and a steep descent

WILDLIFE INTEREST:
Red grouse, ravens, curlew, golden plover. Mountain hare. Cloudberry, heather, bilberry

Cockerels at Upper Booth

This is a short exploration of the southern edges of Kinder Scout from the Vale of Edale. It ascends to the plateau by one of the less-frequented routes and takes in some of the most striking and unusual rock formations, descending by one of the ancient packhorse routes which cross the mountain.

A Upper Booth, Edale 102852
The Vale of Edale is punctuated by a series of small hamlets which all bear the suffix 'booth'. Booth is an Old Danish word meaning a temporary shelter usually used by stockmen, and Edale has five, from the head of the valley: Upper Booth, Barber Booth, Grindsbrook Booth (now usually known as Edale village), Ollerbrook Booth and Nether Booth.

Once threatened by the construction of a steel works, Edale is now the centre for Dark Peak walkers, standing as it does in the shadow of the Peak's highest hill, Kinder Scout. Miraculously, it is still served by a railway – the Hope Valley line – which was built in 1894 to link Sheffield and Manchester. This is still known as 'the Ramblers' Route' and many walkers still use the service to come out into the heart of the High Peak from the neighbouring cities.

a Park at the large lay-by just beyond the railway bridge past Whitmore Lea Farm, Barber Booth, on the minor dalehead road (GR 108847). Continue up the road which leads into the National Trust hamlet of Upper Booth. Take the footpath which leads right just after crossing the bridge over the River Noe, and ascend on a narrow path through the trees above Crowden Brook. The path keeps just below the wall and heads almost due north towards the impending hills.

b Cross a delightful footbridge in a rowan-shaded hollow and ascend the opposite bank of the clough which now assumes the character of a Highland glen. The path works along the side of the clough before descending to the brook as it narrows.

c Soon the great buttress of Crowden Tower, looking like a medieval castle, appears on the skyline to the left, and as the valley narrows still further, you must choose the best route

The Woolpacks (the Moat Stone)

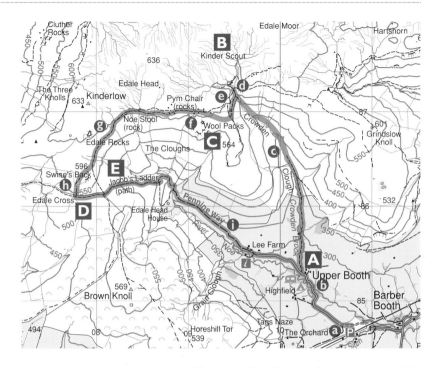

you can, scrambling over boulders and criss-crossing the stream. Please note rocks are slippery when wet. (The easiest route slants up the hillside to the left away from the stream to reach the plateau to the right of Crowden Tower.)

B Kinder Scout 095872

Kinder Scout is a 39km²/15 sq. mile morass of peat bogs, haggs (banks) and groughs (channels) which constitutes the highest ground in the Peak District. Nowhere does it fall much lower than the 610m/2,000ft mark, and is the highest ground in England south of the Yorkshire Dales.

It is still misleadingly marked on some maps as 'The Peak' but anything less like a 'sharply pointed hill' in the dictionary definition would be difficult to find. It probably takes its name from Kinder Downfall on the western flank, but the name now covers the entire mountain. It is probably the most walked-on mountain in Britain, and is often seriously underestimated by those who do not know its navigational intricacies and sudden weather changes.

d Turn left and scramble up the rocks to admire the view from the top of Crowden Tower, which extends down the

Walking amongst the Woolpacks

Crowden Brook

Please note: time taken calculated according to the Naismith formula (see p.2)

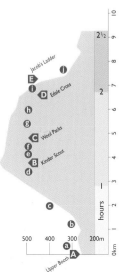

steep-sided Crowden Clough to the long, gulley-split line of Rushup Edge across the valley of the Noe to the south.

e   Take the broad perimeter path which leads between banks of peat towards the next objective, the curious collection of rocks known as the Wool Packs.

C   The Wool Packs 091869

These extraordinary tors have several highly-descriptive alternative names, from the Mushroom Garden to Whipsnade, but I prefer the original of the Wool Packs, so-called because of their resemblance to the bulbous packs of wool carried by the packhorse trains. Formed by countless aeons of erosion by wind, rain and frost, these rounded tors of slightly harder gritstone compare with Brimham Rocks in their exotic and picturesque shapes. Some have earned their own names, like the Moat Stone, surrounded by water; the Anvil; the Pagoda; and Pym Chair, perhaps named after the Puritan leader. Sculptor Henry Moore is said to have taken his inspiration for his monumental works from natural forms such as these.

f After a thorough exploration, leave these fantastic rocks and pass the huge throne-like Pym's Chair on your right and head west again on the perimeter track across the headwaters of the River Noe towards the prominent 'anvil' of Noe Stool. (The earliest maps of Kinder Scout describe it as 'Noe Stool Hill).

g Beyond Noe Stool the path follows the remains of a wall down and around the side of Swine's Back Hill. Keep the wall on your left until you reach another wall. Turn left down the side of the wall to a gate by Edale Cross which is over the wall on your right.

D Edale Cross 077861
This ancient boundary mark, now incongruously enclosed by a three-sided wall, may have originally been erected to define the lands of Basingwerk Abbey in Wales as early as the 12th century, even though it bears the date mark of 1610. It was re-erected by local farmers in 1810 (the initials 'JG' refer to one of them, John Gee), before the National Trust encased it in the unnecessary walling more recently. It must have guided the way for countless generations of travellers crossing this western shoulder of Kinder Scout.

h From the cross turn eastwards down the track to its junction with the Pennine Way at another gate. Carry on downwards to the Head of Jacob's Ladder, which has gained some unfortunately urban-looking walling and paving in recent years.

E Jacob's Ladder 087862
This famous staircase climbing out of the head of the Edale valley is said to have been constructed by one Jacob Marshall. Marshall was an 17th century packhorse trader of Edale Head House (now ruined) who cut this short-cut route up the hillside for himself, while his laden pony took the longer, zig-zag route, which can still be seen over to the right. The route

Walking towards Jacob's Ladder

was reconstructed by the National Trust in the late 1980s after it had suffered serious erosion, and now forms part of the re-aligned Pennine Way. The pretty little packhorse bridge which crosses the Noe at the foot of the incline is known as Yongate Bridge.

i   It is now an easy stroll along the track which leads down past Lee Farm back to Upper Booth, with the heights of Brown Knoll, cut by the ravine of Grain Clough, across the Noe to the right.

KINDER DOWNFALL

START/FINISH:
Hayfield, served by buses from Glossop and Stockport. Buses also call at Hayfield from New Mills which is on the Sheffield–Manchester railway line

DISTANCE:
About 13km/8 miles

APPROXIMATE TIME:
Allow 5–6 hours

HIGHEST POINT:
Kinder Low, 633m/2,077ft

MAPS:
OS Outdoor Leisure Sheet 1, The Dark Peak; Harveys Dark Peak North

REFRESHMENTS:
Pubs and cafes in Hayfield

ADVICE:
A strenuous moorland ramble for which waterproofs, map and compass are essential

WILDLIFE INTEREST:
Red grouse, merlin, raven, golden plover. Mountain hare, fox

Kinder Downfall from Hayfield is one of the classic Dark Peak outings, and the early part of the walk follows the route of the famous Mass Trespass of April, 1932, so gaining an historic importance in the history of the access movement. The western side of Kinder Scout is in many respects the most spectacular, and the Downfall is one of the most impressive landforms in the entire district.

A   Hayfield 048869

Mercifully by-passed by the A624, Hayfield has regained some of its tranquillity but it is still a bustling little township whose history goes back to the wealth won from the woollen, cotton, paper and calico printing industries. It also stood at the hub of various packhorse trails setting out to cross the wilds of Kinder Scout, from where the River Kinder joins the Sett, sometimes in tumultuous fashion. In 1818, the church was swept away by a flood and it was rebuilt in its present classical Georgian style. Hayfield is a perfect little Pennine town, founded on industry and now popular in its 'retirement' for commuters to Manchester and Stockport.

Walking from Hayfield to Kinder
showing Kinder Reservoir

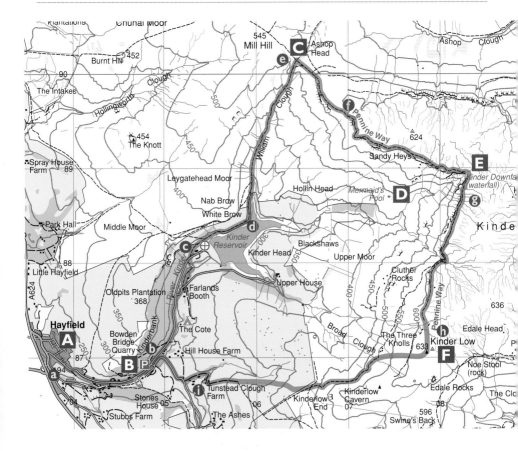

a Take the Kinder Road which climbs up out of Hayfield to the east past the Packhorse public house – last watering place for the packhorse 'jaggers' crossing Kinder – with the River Kinder down to the right. After 800m/½ mile on this lane you pass the Bowden Bridge Quarry (now a car park) on your left.

B Bowden Bridge Quarry 048870

A brass plaque set into the wall of this small gritstone quarry states simply that the Mass Trespass onto Kinder Scout started here on April 24, 1932. About 400 ramblers (the numbers vary according to which account you read) gathered here after the 'mass trespass' had been advertised in Manchester newspapers. They were incensed that they were still not allowed to ramble freely on the highest ground in the Peak District, which was strictly preserved by the grouse-shooting landowners, and were determined to force the issue. An unemployed mechanic called Benny Rothman was pressed into addressing the crowd from a ledge in the quarry, and then they set off, singing cheerfully, for Kinder. At a pre-arranged signal as they ascended William Clough, they broke ranks and ascended the open moor below Sandy Heys, where they were met by a small force of gamekeepers. In the ensuing melee, one gamekeeper was slightly injured, and several ramblers were arrested when they returned to Hayfield. Five of them later received prison sentences for riotous assembly, but the point had been made. The rambling establishment was united for the first time, and when the National Park was formed in 1951, access agreements were negotiated with the landowners.

b Our route follows that taken by the trespassers along Kinder Road swinging right over the bridge and left to a footpath sign where we pick up the riverside path. At the end turn left up to a gate giving access to a steep paved path signed 'Footpath to Open Country'. This heads up and swings sharp left to the symbolic 'Access to Open Country' gate on White Brow.

c Here there are lovely views across the sparkling water of the Kinder Reservoir towards our objective, the deep defile of Kinder Downfall, ahead and to the left on the skyline.

d Rounding Nab Brow, the path contours around the entrance to William Clough, which is said to have been named after a medieval metal-worker who had a smelting works here. You now ascend the clough, crossing and re-crossing the stream as the path demands eventually coming to a tricky, badly-eroded, shale section near the top which leads to the cross-roads of paths beneath Ashop Head, which towers to your right.

C Ashop Head and the Pennine Way 066899

The beautifully-restored natural stone-set staircase which leads up to the westernmost buttress of Kinder Scout is an award-winning example of unobtrusive footpath restoration. The work was carried out by the National Trust, working with the National Park Authority and the Countryside Commission, which is responsible for the Pennine Way National Trail.

The Pennine Way, which runs 435km/270 miles from Edale to Kirk Yetholm, opened in 1965 and was the brainchild of access campaigner Tom Stephenson. His 'hidden agenda' behind the idea of a 'long green trail' up the Pennines was to open up the then forbidden moorlands, particularly in the

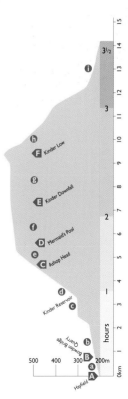

Please note: time taken calculated according to the Naismith formula (see p.2)

Peak District and South Pennines. Today it is still Britain's most popular long-distance footpath, attempted by over 10,000 people a year. But with its popularity have come severe problems of erosion, especially in soft peat country like Kinder, Bleaklow and Black Hill. Hence the need for the kind of remedial work seen at Ashop Head. The National Park Authority now employs a full-time team of footpath restorers which purely works on the Pennine Way.

e Turn right to climb the 'staircase' at Ashop Head, and now follow the line of the Pennine Way southwards, as it keeps to the edge of the plateau, passing Sandy Heys, and swinging left through the peat between rocky outcrops with the glinting eye of the Mermaid's Pool on the boulder-strewn moor beneath.

D   Mermaid's Pool 074886

This dark, reedy little mountain tarn has, as its name and isolated situation might suggest, many legends attached to it. Local people used to believe that if you went to the pool on Easter Eve, you would see a beautiful mermaid and thus be granted the gift of eternal life. But before you scoff at the idea, one 19th century Hayfield resident, Aaron Ashton, was a frequent visitor to the pool and he lived to the ripe old age of 104!

f Continue on the path towards the increasingly-impressive rocky amphitheatre of Kinder Downfall, which is reached through more wind-eroded tors.

E   Kinder Downfall 083889

This 30m/100ft high waterfall is the biggest in the Peak District, and a landmark on the Pennine Way. The Kinder River drops off the plateau here, but in summer, is never more than a disappointing trickle. In wet weather, however, the Downfall is impressive, especially when a westerly wind funnels up the valley and blows the water back as a shifting, hanging curtain in the air. This is one of the best-known spectacles of the Peak, and in the right conditions can be seen as far away as Stockport. In winter, the waterfall can be transformed into a shimmering curtain of ice, attracting ice-climbers to one of their very few opportunities in the Peak.

The Downfall is probably the feature which gave the entire mountain its name. On old maps, it is the area around the Downfall which is known as Kinder Scout, and the name, which may be Norse, has been translated to 'water falling over a projecting cliff', which is a pretty accurate description.

Golden plover

It is also a popular lunchspot for all Kinder walkers which attract a band of voracious sheep who are not above pinching your sandwiches when you are not looking!

g   Turn south from the Downfall following the well-trodden line of the Pennine Way which swings around the chasm of Red Brook, which neatly frames the Mermaid's Pool and then, taking the left-hand fork of the path, follow a series of cairns until the white trig point of Kinder Low appears ahead perched on a rock surrounded by bare peat.

F   Kinder Low 079870

Kinder Low at (633m/2,077ft) is only 3m/11ft lower – and a lot easier to find – than the actual summit of Kinder Scout. It sits in a desert-like expanse of wind-blown peat and sand, the result of years of over-grazing, moorland fires and wind and acid-rain erosion. John Hillaby must have been thinking of Kinder Low when he described Kinder as a land in botanical terms 'at the end of its tether'.

h   As you are on access land you can cut down across the open moor from Kinder Low to the prominent rocks of the Three Knolls due west to join the path which leads up from Tunstead Clough Farm. This leads down beneath Kinderlow End to the intake wall and access point.

i   Crossing a series of stiles, you go around Tunstead Clough Farm and easily down by its access road to Bowden Bridge. You then turn left to descend down the Kinder Road back into Hayfield.

DERWENT EDGE

Fairholmes, beneath the wall of the Derwent Dam, is the
natural magnet for visitors to the Upper Derwent Valley.
But to see the real drama of the valley it is necessary to
head for the heights of Derwent Edge, and this all-day
moorland walk takes in most of the startling series of tors and
cloughs which punctuate this peaty promenade.

A   Fairholmes 172892

Originally a farm built where Lockerbrook ran into the River
Derwent, Fairholmes was used as a mason's workyard while
the Derwent and Howden Dams were under construction
between 1901 and 1917. The lower car park was used as a
tree nursery for the extensive forestry plantations which now
cloak the valley sides.

The construction of the Derwent and Howden Dams was a
major feat of civil engineering, and involved the building of a
railway which brought the stone for the dams from quarries at
Grindleford. The navvies lived in a workmens' village at
Birchinlee, which housed over 1,000 people for the period of
construction. Known as 'Tin Town' because most of the
temporary, portable buildings were made of corrugated iron,
Birchinlee was a self-contain community with its own school,
hospital, community hall and post office. Nothing no remains
but a few foundations lost in the conifers. There is a National
Park visitor centre at Fairholmes which tells the story of the
valley.

Autumn reflections around
Derwent Reservoir

Derwent Dam in full flood

a   Take the road which leads down from Fairholmes and beneath the formidable Derwent Dam wall which, in times of high rainfall, overflows in an awesome, thunderous waterfall. From the right-hand corner of the dam wall, steps lead up through the trees to the perimeter track around the Derwent Reservoir.

B   Derwent Reservoir 170910

The Derwent and Howden Reservoirs were built by the Derwent Valley Water Board to supply water to the thirsty cities of Derby, Nottingham, Leicester and Sheffield. The Derwent was the second to be completed in 1916, and was the scene in the Second World War of training runs by the famous 617 Squadron, 'the Dambusters', in preparation for their epic attack on the Ruhr Valley dams in 1943. The terrain of the Upper Derwent and the twin-towered dams were apparently the closest models for the Moehne and Eder Dams in Germany. Regular reunions and flypasts still take place over the Derwent Dam, attracting huge crowds of people, remembering this daring and fateful raid.

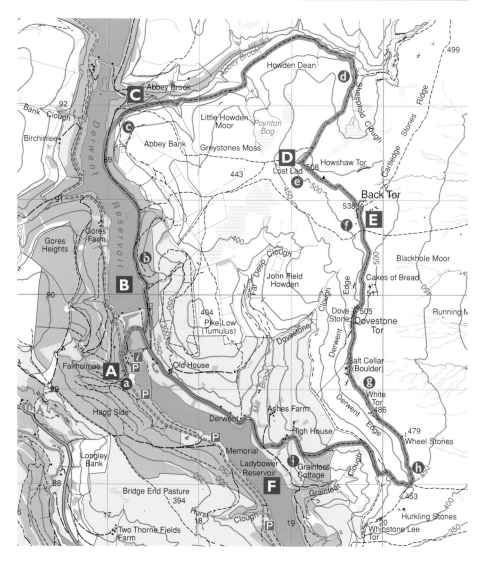

b The route continues along the shoreline road through the trees of Shireowlers Wood until the towers of Howden Reservoir appear ahead. The track descends towards the Abbey Brook bridge but we turn right (signpost) to enter the confines of Abbey Brook itself.

C Abbey Brook 172921

This deep clough which bites into the Howden Moors takes its name from a former 'grange' of Welbeck Abbey in far-off

Nottinghamshire. The daffodils which spring into life annually here are said to have been planted by these medieval monks who doubled as sheep farmers. Their convent was situated close to the Ladybower Inn on the A57, and gave its name to that area of the Derwent Valley ('Lady's Bower').

c   Follow this track which soon leaves the trees and leads into open country at a gate. This is a glorious high-level shooter's track, narrow in places, which leads into the heart of the moors, crossing Cogman Clough and the aptly-named Wild Moor Clough on the way. Ahead, the crags of Berristers Tor seem to block the way where the clough narrows, but it is by-passed by the dog-leg around Sheepfold Clough.

d   Turn right here into Sheepfold Clough and climb out onto the open moor. You need to bear to the right of Howshaw Tor, heading for the prominent hill top of Lost Lad Hillend. It is a few steps now on a paved track south east from here to reach Lost Lad itself.

D   Lost Lad 193912
The intriguing name of this fine 518m/1,700ft viewpoint comes from the tale of a young shepherd boy who was lost on these moors while gathering sheep one snowy winter's day. Search parties were sent out, but his frozen body was not found until the following spring by a shepherd who saw the words 'Lost Lad' scratched on an adjacent rock by the desperate boy. There is a memorial toposcope on the summit erected by the famous Sheffield Clarion Ramblers, showing across the deep gash of the Derwent Win Hill, the Mam Tor ridge and the eastern end of Kinder Scout.

e   A broad paved track, installed by the National Trust to combat erosion, now runs the short distance towards the prominent rocky summit of Back Tor, with its white trig. point cemented onto the highest point and requiring a little scrambling to reach it. It is well worth the effort, for this is one of the finest and wildest viewpoints in the entire Dark Peak.

E   Back Tor 197910
For John Derry, author of the bogtrotter's classic Across the Derbyshire Moors first published in 1926, the summit of Back Tor was one of his favourite places: And yet it does one good to get into this upland, age-long solitude, where the primeval world is felt to be a mighty fact, linked on to us. The spirit of the moors has his throne on Back Tor.

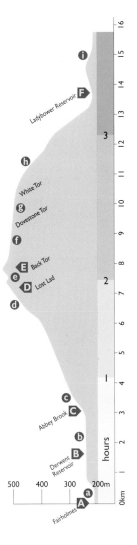

Please note: time taken calculated according to the Naismith formula (see p.2)

The 538m/1,765ft summit may not be one of the highest points of the Dark Peak, but for sheer wildness it takes some beating, with not a sign of human habitation to be seen. The view extends north to the wilderness of Bleaklow and the head of the Derwent Valley, and south west to the Kinder plateau. To the south there's a glimpse of the Ladybower Reservoir and Win Hill pushes its craggy top to break the horizon at the end of the Great Ridge, while to the east across Strines can be seen the white tower blocks of the city of Sheffield.

f　Go south on another flagged path through the peat and heather towards the next outcrop which is picturesquely known as the Cakes of Bread. Dovestone Tor is the next of these eroded remains of slightly harder gritstone which have survived the ravages of aeons of wind, frost and rain. Keep heading south, and the still-paved path takes you to one of the most celebrated of these weirdly-shaped tors so obvious from Derwent Lane – the anvil-shaped Salt Cellar which stands in glorious isolation in a sea of heather.

g　Keep on the edge path which crosses White Tor and heads towards the prominent large outcrop known on the map as the Wheel Stones but locally and much more accurately as the Coach and Horses. Viewed on the horizon from the Strines Road, this is exactly what they look like.

The Salt Cellar

h　Just below the Coach and Horses at the cross-roads of the edge track and the bridlepath from Moscar, turn right to reach the boundary of open country at a gate, and follow this down above a plantation wall to Grindle Clough, past a collection of ancient barns, one of which has a lintel dated 1647. From the barns, the path is again rather incongruously paved as it leads down to the eastern shore of Ladybower Reservoir.

F　Ladybower Reservoir 190880

The Ladybower was the last of the Derwent Reservoirs to be built, between 1935 and 1943, and it involved the depopulation of the twin villages of Ashopton and Derwent – the famous 'drowned villages' of the Derwent. In times of drought, the foundations of Derwent village are sometimes revealed in the reservoir floor around here, and thousands of people, including some former inhabitants, come to wonder at them. The Ladybower Reservoir was formally opened by King George VI in 1945.

i   It is now a simple matter of turning right on the eastern perimeter track to walk the last 1.6km/1 mile back to Fairholmes, passing the gateposts to Derwent Hall and what remains of Derwent village en route, now a few scattered farmsteads around a telephone box, and eventually beneath the towers of the Derwent Dam again.

Path at the top of Grindle Clough

AROUND LANGSETT TO NORTH AMERICA

START/FINISH:
Yorkshire Water's Langsett Barn car park on the A616 Stocksbridge-Flouch road. Served by buses from Sheffield and Stocksbridge

DISTANCE:
8km/5 miles

APPROXIMATE TIME:
Allow about 3 hours

HIGHEST POINT:
Hingcliff Hill 327m/1,073ft

MAPS:
OS Outdoor Leisure Sheet 1, The Dark Peak; Harveys, Dark Peak North

REFRESHMENTS:
Pubs and cafe in Langsett

ADVICE:
Forest tracks followed by moorland paths, boots required. Take care in poor weather/visibility

WILDLIFE INTEREST:
Siskins and goldcrest in forestry; red grouse, golden plover and merlin on moors. Gulls, great crested grebe and other waterfowl on reservoir. Badger and fox in woods

The conversion of Langsett Barn, a magnificent 17th century building, to a visitor centre, ranger base and community centre for the village of Langsett in 1993 was an excellent example of co-operation between local authorities and a water company. It has opened up a largely unknown area of the National Park to many more visitors for whom this circular walk, taking in the ruined farmstead known as North America, is a popular excursion.

A   Langsett Barn 210004
The village of Langsett gets its name from the Old English for 'long slope', which is a fair description of the way that the village sits where the Midhope Moors slope down to the Porter, or Little Don, River (one of the few rivers in Britain with two official names).

The chief feature of Langsett today is the reservoir, which was built between 1889 and 1904 by an army of navvies who lived in a temporary village of corrugated iron huts beneath the dam wall, which included a hospital, canteen and recreation rooms.

a   Leave the car park at Langsett Barn by the gate which leads down through Langsett Bank Woods to a path which leads right alongside the reservoir. The path rises through a replanted area and you will soon glimpse the stone-built Brookhouse Bridge which spans the Porter or Little Don.

Langsett Reservoir

b   The path now joins the ancient bridleway known as the Cut Gate Track and goes down to cross the bridge.

B   The Cut Gate Track 198006
This ancient track was used by farmers in the Upper Derwent and Woodlands Valley to take their livestock to the nearest market, which was at Penistone. The Cut Gate track runs from the reconstructed Slippery Stones bridge at the head of the Howden Reservoir up Bull Clough and over Featherbed Moss to Mickleden Edge before dropping over Hingcliff Hill into Langsett. Stone Age arrowheads have been found in the peat close to the Cut Gate track, so it seems that these now bleak and inhospitable moors have seen signs of human activity for many thousands of years.

Lichen-covered rock in Langsett Bank Woods

Near the bridge are the remains of Brookhouse Farm, which was one of several which were depopulated in the interests of water purity when the reservoir was built at the start of the 20th century. In 1588, so a story says, the rent for this farm was a red rose at Christmas and a snowball at midsummer!

c   Cross the bridge and go through the gate up the hillside opposite on the track which soon leaves the trees behind and enters open moorland at Delf Edge. The way now climbs steadily over Hingcliff Common towards Hingcliff Hill, the high point of the walk.

d   Where the path forks, take the left hand path which leads down, with views across the reservoir to the ruins of an old farmstead.

C   North America Farm 203997
In the days when the Empire was being opened up, it was the custom to name far-flung farmsteads after the places which were, in those days, on the edge of the known world. That is how North America got its name; other farms were called Quebec and Botany Bay. It is a sad ruin now, like Brookhouse Farm it was abandoned when the reservoir was built. You might notice the pockmarks in some of the stones of the broken-down walls. These were caused when the ruined farm was used for target practice by troops in training for the D-Day landings in the Second World War, who were stationed near Langsett.

e   From the farm ruins, go down the track back towards the reservoir, keeping the conifers of Mauk Royd on your left, and crossing Thickwoods Brook, which enters the reservoir from

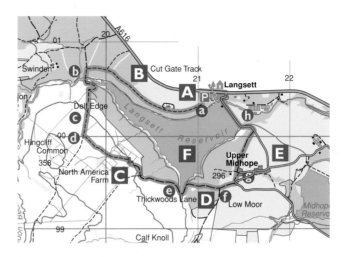

the right. Passing through a metal gate, you should note the fine views to the left up towards the head of the reservoir. You now enter Thickwoods Lane with Thickwoods Plantation to your right.

D   Thickwoods Lane 210995
Thickwoods Lane was reinforced to accommodate tanks during the Second World War, probably for the Army training mentioned above which used the area around North America Farm. The brick rubble from which the track is made came from bombed out houses in nearby Sheffield.

f   Through another gate, you reach a concrete track across which is a metal barrier. Go through the gap in the wall and turn left up a walled green lane which leads to the hamlet of Townend, which is part of the hamlet of Upper Midhope.

E   Upper Midhope 216996
The twin villages of Midhopestones and Upper Midhope are linked by Midhope Lane, and are of very ancient origin. 'Hope' is an Old English word meaning 'a small, enclosed valley', which is still a very good topographical description of the area. The tiny church of St. James at Midhopestones was restored in 1705, and has a fine, much earlier Renaissance pulpit.

Across the valley of the Little Don from Upper Midhope, around Alderman's Head Farm, the lost market town of Penisale once existed. It was granted the right to hold a market as early as 1290, but nothing now remains.

Remains of North America Farm

g Turn left and then right through Townend and take the bridleway down to meet Joseph Lane until it joins the road. Turn left at the road to the pavement which crosses the embankment wall of the Langsett Reservoir.

F   Langsett Reservoir 213002

The embankment of Langsett Reservoir is 352m/1,156 ft long and has a depth of 35m/117ft. to the old river bed beneath. When full, the reservoir holds 59 million m³ or 1,409 million gallons of water. The castellated valvehouse at the northern end of the dam wall is supposed to have been modelled on the gatehouse of Lancaster Castle. The reservoir took 14 years to build, between 1889 and 1904.

The reservoir is now controlled by Yorkshire Water, and its naturally acidic, brown water is treated at the modern Langsett Treatment Works just below the embankment wall to the right.

h Reaching the junction with the A616 opposite the Bank View Café, turn left and left again along a lane which leads past a large barn on your right. Turn left between two walls to return to the Langsett Barn car park.

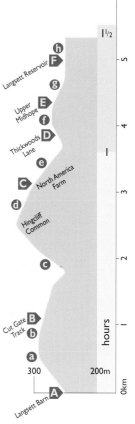

Please note: time taken calculated according to the Naismith formula (see p.2)

BLEAKLOW

START/FINISH:
Old Glossop

DISTANCE:
14km/9 miles

APPROXIMATE TIME:
Allow at least 5–6 hours

HIGHEST POINT:
Bleaklow Head 633m/2,076ft

MAPS:
OS Outdoor Leisure Sheet 1, The Dark Peak; Harveys, Dark Peak North

REFRESHMENTS:
In Glossop

ADVICE:
An extremely tough moorland ramble; waterproofs, map and compass essential. This route should only be undertaken by experienced and well-eqipped walkers, competent with map and compass

WILDLIFE INTEREST:
Red grouse, golden plover, twite, curlew, meadow pipit, fox, mountain hare

There are many approaches to Bleaklow's wild and isolated summit, but this one from the old cotton town of Glossop is one of the most satisfying. The second highest hill in the Peak never gets the same number of walkers as Kinder and its devotees are grateful for that, for Bleaklow still manages to convey a feeling of remoteness and wildness in a way that over-populated Kinder cannot. Please note many sections of this walk are pathless and will require the use of a detailed map and compass.

A   Glossop 041948

Glossop's wealth, like that of so many towns west of the Pennines, was founded on King Cotton. The patronage of the 11th Duke of Norfolk gave the centre of the town its fine range of civic buildings and squares, and it is no coincidence that the planned early 19th century streets and factories at the western end of the town were named 'Howardstown' – a reference to the family name.

Bleaklow from Snake Summit

But Old Glossop, the starting point of our walk, was there long before that, a pleasing mixture of old gritstone cottages clustered around the parish church, which sprang up at the junction of packhorse routes preparing to cross the Pennines. Earlier still, the Roman fort of Melandra, north-west of the town now in the huge Gamesley housing estate, guarded the entrance to Longdendale.

a From All Saints Church walk past the Old Cross and turn left along Sheply Street past factories and along a track. This leads to a ladder stile and access point onto the Lightside ridge, with the insalubriously-named Shittern Clough down to the left.

b Keep to this ridge and climb steadily towards the rocks of Yellowslacks ahead. Go along the edge of these rocks, which were once blown up by an irate landowner in a bid to stop climbing on them, above the narrowing Yellowslacks Brook, which soon becomes Dowstone Clough.

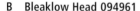

The Wain Stones or Kissing Stones

c Head east-north-east at the end, heading across boggy Shelf Moss towards the Wain Stones. These isolated boulders were made famous by Alfred Wainwright, who first likened two of them when seen from a certain angle, to the profile of a kissing couple.Continue in the same direction until you reach Bleaklow Head.

B Bleaklow Head 094961

Despite its elevation of 633m/2,076ft, the view from the summit rocks of Bleaklow Head is disappointing, considering it is the second highest summit in the Peak. All that can be seen is a wasteland of peat haggs and groughs, with only the

Bleaklow Summit

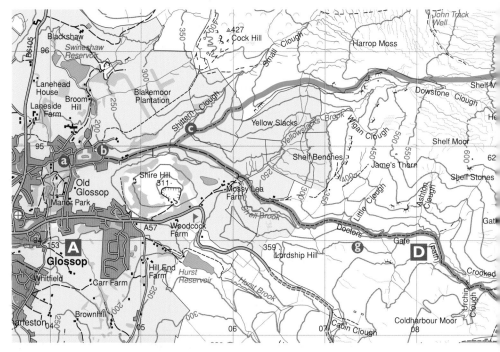

peeping of the occasional meadow pipit or the croaking of a grouse for company. Bleaklow Head stands on the watershed of England, so that the 152cm/60in of rain which falls annually on the summit eventually finds its way into either the Irish Sea, via the Mersey, or the North Sea, via the Humber.

d From Bleaklow Head, turn south-south-west passing the Wain Stones again and head for Hern Stones, whose name may come from the Old English 'earn' meaning eagle. Follow the ridge through the morass of peat groughs south again making for the welcome dry ground and scattered tors surrounding the white trig. point on High Shelf Stones.

C Higher Shelf Stones 089948

This is probably the finest viewpoint on the Bleaklow massif, the bold promontory seen from the Snake Pass just as it starts to drop down into Glossop. At 621m/2,037ft, it looks down on Doctor's Gate across the Shelf Brook valley, and over Coldharbour Moor towards the distant Mill Hill and Chinley Churn, with Shining Tor just peeping over the massive northern shoulder of Kinder Scout.

Along the Pennine Way towards Bleaklow from Doctor's Gate

Higher Shelf Stones was the scene in 1948 of a tragic aircrash involving a U.S. Air Force B29 Superfortress, involved in the Berlin Air Lift. All 13 members of the aircrew were killed, and a simple memorial erected on the 40th anniversary now marks the spot. Just beneath the summit to the east there are still large pieces of wreckage to be seen, and there are stories of ghostly apparitions having been seen near the spot.

e   Descend from Higher Shelf Stones in a south-easterly direction across Gathering Hill – a reference to a sheep gathering ground – until you meet the line of the engineered path which is the Pennine Way at Devil's Dyke. This is an ancient boundary ditch, possibly dating from the Dark Ages.

f   After about 800m/½ mile of this pleasurably dryshod route, you meet the ancient causeway known as Doctor's Gate, where you turn right for the long descent back into Glossop.

D   Doctor's Gate 090933

Marked on the map as a 'Roman Road,' the stones on this ancient track are probably a medieval packhorse route, built on the line of a much older Roman route between the forts of *Melandra* near Glossop, and *Navio*, at Brough in the Hope Valley.

It is thought to get its name from Dr. John Talbot, the vicar of Glossop between 1494 and 1550, who must have been a frequent traveller on this moorland route.

g   The route is now obvious and gradually descends the Doctor's Gate path across Urchin Clough, Rose Clough and Birchin Orchard Clough on a superb natural route. Doctor's Gate eventually joins the valley of the Shelf Brook, crossing Yellowslacks Brook near Mossy Lea Farm, and rejoins the outward route and back into Old Glossop.

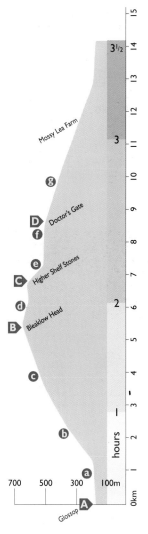

Please note: time taken calculated according to the Naismith formula (see p.2)

BLACK HILL AND THE CROWDEN HORSESHOE

START/FINISH:
Crowden-in-Longdendale car park, Longdendale. Occasional buses in summer

DISTANCE:
14.5km/9 miles

APPROXIMATE TIME:
Allow at least 5 hours

HIGHEST POINT:
Black Hill, 582m/1,908ft

MAPS:
OS Outdoor Leisure Sheet 1, The Dark Peak; Harveys, Dark Peak North

REFRESHMENTS:
At Crowden

ADVICE:
A strenuous moorland walk for which good waterproof equipment and a compass (and knowledge of how to use it) are required. Ground and weather conditions can be extreme

WILDLIFE INTEREST:
Red grouse, merlin, peregrine falcon, golden plover. Fox, mountain hare

Wainwright somewhat unkindly dubbed Longdendale 'Manchester-in-the-Country', and it must be admitted that this major trans-Pennine valley has suffered more than most from the hand of Man. Although it is flooded by a string of five reservoirs, threaded by the busy A628 trunk road and defiled by an army of marching electricity pylons, Longdendale's enclosing moors retain their wild beauty, as this walk shows.

A   Crowden-in-Longdendale 072992

Crowden has always been an important stop-over place for travellers using the Woodhead Pass and entering Longdendale. Crowden Hall, a fine late 17th century Stuart mansion, was demolished in 1937 by the Manchester Waterworks Company in the interests of preserving water purity. Crowden had its own railway station on the Woodhead line on the opposite side of the valley, and the last remaining terraced cottages, known as Long Row, were converted by the National Park to a much-needed first-stop youth hostel on the soon-to-be-opened Pennine Way in 1964.

When the string of five reservoirs which now fill the valley bottom were constructed between 1848 and 1877, they formed the greatest man-made expanse of water in the world, and were praised as a wonderful example of Victorian engineering. The Bottoms, Valehouse, Rhodeswood, Torside and Woodhead Reservoirs were needed to provide pure drinking water for the fast-expanding industrial population of Manchester.

a   From the car park, pass the camp site which was built on the site of Crowden Hall and turn left through a gate and over Crowden Brook Bridge. Through a second gate, you turn right to join the Pennine Way, over a ladder stile by a small plantation.

b   Turn left and follow the well-beaten path towards Black Tor, noting Rotherham's Outdoor Pursuits Centre down to the right. Continue left around the edge of the moorland crossing a small stream (Span Gutter) beneath Black Tor and ascend gradually towards the lovely moorland stream of Oakenclough Brook. The path thins as it climbs towards the impressive

buttresses of Laddow Rocks ahead. Beyond Laddow Rocks, the prominent twin landslipped hillocks known as The Castles defend the head of the valley, with Black Hill beyond. Take the edge path, ignoring the left-hand branch to Chew Reservoir, to reach the summit rocks of Laddow.

Cotton grass on Black Hill

B   Laddow Rocks 057015

Laddow Rocks hold an important place in the history of rock climbing in the Peak. They were among the first crags to be explored by Manchester climbers in the early years of the 20th century, long before Stanage and Froggatt were 'discovered'. Climbers used to sleep in the cave below the rocks to get an early start, and some climbs were done wearing clogs, or even in bare feet!

Laddow also saw the start of the mountain rescue service in the Peak. Following a serious accident on the rocks in 1928, a climber was carried off and down to Crowden using a pair of 'No Trespassers' signposts as a make-shift stretcher. This incident led to the formation of the 'Joint Stretcher Committee' in 1933, which was the predecessor of the modern Peak District Mountain Rescue Organisation.

c   The path continues northwards along the edge of the rocks, then gradually runs down towards Crowden Great

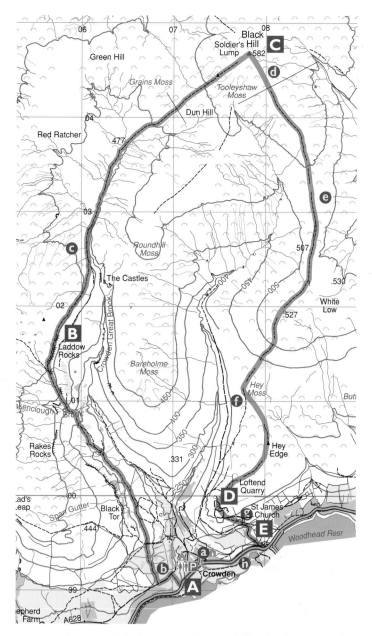

Brook, near the twin rocky outcrops of The Castles across the stream. Keep on this peaty and often boggy path below Red Ratcher, to the left, and gradually ascend across Grains Moss until it levels out at Dun Hill. The summit of Black Hill, marked by its stranded white trig point, is now ahead, but can only be reached by negotiating an unpleasant quagmire of cloying peat.

C Black Hill 078047

Wainwright didn't think much of Black Hill either. 'It is not the only fell (sic) with a summit of peat, but no other shows such a desolate and hopeless quagmire to the sky'.

Formerly the highest point of the old county of Cheshire (most of Longdendale fell within that county), Black Hill at 582m/1,908ft is entirely appropriately named. It really is black and in the usually-soggy conditions which exist here, it is a formidable challenge to the hillwalker to reach the isolated trig point, stranded high above the level of the surrounding sea of fast-eroding peat, and keep his or her socks dry.

The official name of the summit is 'Soldier's Lump', a reference to the 18th century visits of the Royal Engineer surveyors who first used it as a triangulation point. An examination of the mound in 1841 revealed the timber framework for the theodolite which was used for the survey, which began in 1784. The original instrument is now in the Science Museum.

The views from Black Hill, on a good day, extend as far as the distant fells of the Yorkshire Dales to the north. Closer at hand, our route is revealed to Laddow Rocks, and the thin needle of the Holme Moss TV mast threads the clouds to the east.

d Leave the summit in a south-easterly direction on a thin path which thankfully leads across drier ground on a series of cairns which leads across Tooleyshaw Moss towards some prominent grouse shooting butts.

e Continue on the broad ridge to White Low and Westend Moss, with its little reedy tarn on the summit plateau. You now begin the gradual descent back down into Longdendale, with the heights of Bleaklow filling the southern horizon across Torside Reservoir.

f Head for the trig point at the summit of Hey Moss, and then follow the ridge down to the top of Loftend Quarry, a prominent, if unsightly, landmark in the Longdendale Valley. The paths in this section are indistinct.

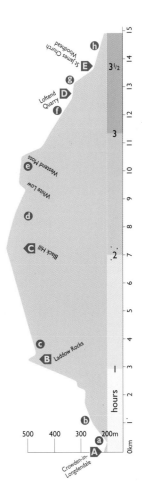

D   Loftend Quarry 075998

This large abandoned quarry with its large spoil heaps is known locally as Moses Quarry – perhaps after a former worker there? In its heyday, it employed 100 men, an indication of the size of the former population of Crowden and the rest of the valley. Stone was produced to provide kerbstones for the fast-growing city of Sheffield. Today, it is popular with rock climbers and the home of some quite rare birds of prey. Plantations have been established in the quarry bottom to help soften the painfully-visible scar.

g   From the quarry descend carefully to the cobbled track below, which winds down to the tiny chapel of St. James by the side of the A628 in the valley bottom.

E   St. James Church, Woodhead 079995

This tiny little church, usually known as Woodhead Chapel, is perhaps best know for its gravestones at the back of the churchyard to many of the navvies who lost their lives during

Crowden Great Brook

Isolated trig point on summit of Black Hill

the terrible cholera outbreak which occurred in 1849 as they were building the second of the Woodhead railway tunnels. Twenty eight men died during the outbreak, adding to the death toll of 33 who were killed making the first, single-track tunnel between 1838 and 1845. It gave Woodhead the reputation as the railwayman's graveyard.

h   On reaching the church turn right down onto the A628 to walk the 800m/½ mile back to Crowden.

COLLINS *rambler's guide*

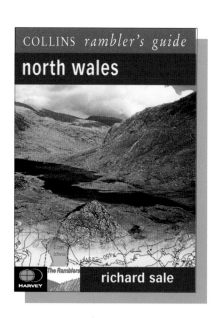

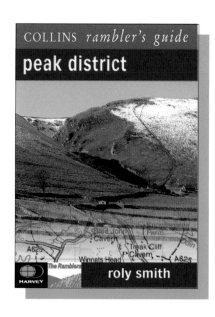

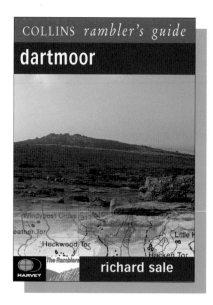